Katie Piper is a ... ...er. In 2008, she survived an attack and ... ...ated Channel 4 documentary *Katie: My Beautiful Face* was watched by 3.5 million viewers and shown in more than fifteen countries. Katie founded her own charity, The Katie Piper Foundation, to help people living with burns and scars and she has received numerous awards and accolades for her charity work, including a prestigious Woman of the Year Award. She is now a presenter on Channel 4 and the author of six books: *Beautiful*, *Things Get Better*, *Start Your Day with Katie*, *Beautiful Ever After*, *Confidence* and *From Mother to Daughter*.

'Katie is one of the most inspirational people I have ever met'
Simon Cowell

'An inspiring read about her journey back to health and how true confidence is far more than skin-deep . . . warm, funny and down-to-earth'
Sun

'Katie Piper is an extraordinary woman'
Mail on Sunday

'Katie's account of her experiences is unflinching, but marked with a deeply impressive dignity and courage'
Daily Mail

'Warm and instantly likeable, Katie Piper has the attitude to life we should all try to emulate'
Best

Also by Katie Piper

Beautiful
Things Get Better
Start Your Day with Katie
Beautiful Ever After
Confidence
From Mother to Daughter

Katie Piper
Confidence

Quercus

First published in Great Britain in 2016 by Quercus Editions Ltd
This paperback edition published in 2017 by

Quercus Editions Ltd
Carmelite House
50 Victoria Embankment
London EC4Y 0DZ

An Hachette UK company

A CIP catalogue record for this book is available
from the British Library

ISBN 978 1 78429 520 2

10 9 8 7 6 5 4 3 2 1

Editorial Consultant: Caro Handley
Psychological Consultant: Christine Webber

Text designed and typeset by CC Book Production

Printed and bound in the UK by Clays Ltd, St Ives plc

I dedicate this book to the Katie Piper Foundation family – staff, trustees, volunteers and survivors. For me you represent true confidence, and through your work with the KPF, you have given the gift of confidence to so many other people, myself included. Thank you for being you.

Contents

Introduction

Confidence – true, deep-down, confidence – is a wonderful thing. It's something everyone deserves to have in bucketloads and yet it's that elusive quality that so many of us feel we are still searching for.

Who hasn't found themselves facing the nerve-wracking prospect of a first date, an interview or some form of public-speaking and thought, 'If only I had more confidence'? Which usually translates into, 'If only I could feel as if I know what I'm doing, and my stomach would stop doing cartwheels.' Because that's what we often equate with confidence – the ability to be cool, unflappable and capable in any situation.

I've been giving confidence a lot of thought, inevitably, since I decided to write this book, and I believe it's about far more than keeping a cool head or having the courage to give something a go – although those things definitely play a part. I think real confidence is about feeling, deep down inside, that you are OK, and that you will still be OK no matter whether you succeed or fail in the things you set out to do. Confidence is about liking and accepting yourself, feeling comfortable with yourself and knowing that you have a lot to offer, whatever anyone around you says. It is about encouraging yourself, being able to push yourself beyond what is familiar and comfortable, and not giving yourself a hard time if things go wrong.

Small children seem to have natural confidence, along with their wonder at the world and joy in the simplest things. But by the time we get to our teens and then become adults, life's inevitable knocks mean that, for most of us, our natural childhood confidence has given way to plenty of caution, self-doubt and self-criticism.

The good news is that it doesn't have to be like that: it's absolutely possible to build up and enhance your confidence. You can go from 1 to 10 on the confidence scale and achieve things you never thought possible – if you're willing to try doing things that are new and feel unfamiliar. This may seem scary at first, but stick with it, because it works.

I say starting from 'one' and not 'zero' because everyone, even the most shy and retiring person, has a little bit of confidence, even if it's only in one area of their life or in just one type of situation. And that's important, because even that small amount of confidence, like a little seed, can grow and develop into something bigger. Nurture it, feed it, appreciate it, give it light and love, and it will flourish.

I've learned a lot about confidence. I grew up in a loving family that always gave me lots of encouragement and praise, so when I first went to live in London in my early twenties, I was pretty confident and ready to try my luck in a modelling and TV-presenting career. By the time I was 24 I was sharing a flat with friends and beginning to land some good jobs. Everything was looking rosy – until my life as I knew it was destroyed in a few moments when I was beaten and raped by a man I had recently met, and then a cup of industrial-strength acid was thrown into my face.

That was almost nine years ago, and since then I've been on an incredible journey which has taken me from the rock bottom of despair to the happiness that I have today, with my charity, the Katie Piper Foundation, a wonderful husband and our gorgeous little girl.

It sounds straightforward when I put it like that, but actually my journey of recovery has been far from a straight line from Z back up to A. Immediately after the attack, I was left badly scarred, with no sight in one eye and very little in the other. Luckily, this has now improved. I was damaged internally, too, as I'd swallowed some of the acid when it was thrown at me. After the attack I had to be fed through a stomach tube, and I faced dozens of operations, two years in a plastic pressure mask and endless skin grafts and reconstructions.

Life looked pretty hopeless. I had lost everything – my health, my looks, my work, my home in London and my plans and dreams for the future. I couldn't imagine ever going out into the world again, ever working, going on a date or having a family. I thought my life was over and all that was left for me was a bleak and painful existence.

It took me a long time to learn that, as desperate as my situation was, there was a lot that I *did* still have, including a future that I could look forward to. I had my family around me – my parents and my brother and sister – offering love and support. I had wonderful doctors who were doing their best to rebuild and repair my damaged body. And I had the fundamental me – my mind and feelings and personality – which was nothing to do with how I looked on the outside. The attackers had hurt me physically, but they couldn't touch my spirit unless I allowed them to.

The journey from those dark days to the life I have today has been bumpy. I didn't simply find a little more courage, hope and confidence each day; I had good days and bad days – and sometimes terrible days, when I just wanted to give up. But gradually the good days began to outnumber the bad and I came to realise that, while going through the darkest of experiences, I had gained so much that was precious.

Confidence, for me, came in individual moments – the first time I was brave enough to leave the house after coming out of hospital; the first time I dared to put on a beautiful dress again; the first time I sat in a business meeting; the first time I faced an audience to talk about what I had endured and learned. Each time, I was terrified, and each time I had to dig deep to find my nerve, my smile and my self-belief. But every time I did this, I grew a little stronger, a little braver and a little more determined to keep on building a future for myself, to make connections with people, to learn from them and pass on what I had learned.

Of course, there were big setbacks, too. There were times when I was hurt by a thoughtless or cruel comment, when I felt too low to face the world or was knocked back by what seemed like a failure. Being abandoned in a restaurant when I finally ventured out on a date for the first time since the attack – that ranked pretty high in the misery stakes. But what I discovered was that if every time I faced a setback I refused to accept defeat, I would feel just a little bit better, a tiny bit more confident and hopeful. And all those small steps soon add up.

I want everyone to feel confident. Whatever your story, whatever your journey, whatever your personal challenges, confidence is the key to growing stronger, braver and wiser. If you have deep-down confidence, you can take life's knocks and you can get back up and put yourself out there again. You can take in your stride whatever life throws at you and still feel good about yourself, no matter what.

In this book I'll be sharing what I've discovered about confidence in my own life, as well as things I've learned from some amazing women, and men, that I've met along the way.

Some of them took part in a diversity catwalk event dedicated to body image and confidence that I hosted at the Ideal Home Show, in London, in the spring of 2015. The Ideal Home Show, held at Olympia every year, is full of exciting, innovative people and ideas, not just for the home but from the fashion and beauty worlds, too. It was my first year as the show's fashion and beauty ambassador, and I wanted to put on a catwalk event that would inspire a new attitude to fashion and beauty that was all about confidence and acceptance. For me, deciding whether something or someone is beautiful is simply an opinion, one based on what we've been conditioned to think by the people and world around us. So for the diversity catwalk I chose a group of eight women who each represented beauty in their own unique way. I wanted to challenge the audience's view of beauty, and to show that if your spirit is strong and you embrace life's challenges, you are beautiful.

Each of these remarkable women – none of whom had ever been on a catwalk before and all of whom had faced life-changing physical illness or injury – modelled stunning outfits and swimsuits and then walked the runway wearing t-shirts with their biggest body insecurities printed on the back.

The event was a fantastic success. The models, thrown into a totally new situation, were brave and brilliant, and the audience gave them such a warm and appreciative response, cheering and applauding and then queuing up to meet them afterwards, which left them feeling so good. For every one of the models it was a turning point in their own remarkable story, in lives that they have made a success against incredible odds. And the people who came to watch the show wanted to know, how did they do it, how did they overcome those huge obstacles to become happy, successful women? Every one of the models refused to give up or to let themselves be made to feel less-than amazing, and they've all achieved remarkable things. When they felt hopeless, or help-less – and each of them did at times! – they forced themselves to get back up again and carry on.

I'll be telling their stories within this book, and passing on important lessons that they have learned on their own personal confidence journeys. I've also asked beauty expert Jordan Bone to share her inspiring tips; Jordan has overcome extraordinary hurdles to become a hugely successful beauty blogger and video blogger, or vlogger. I've asked a couple of my friends to help out, too: Kamran Bedi and I shared a flat in London back before my attack, and he is now a successful life coach who has taught me so much; Jamie Pound and I met through the Katie Piper Foundation and he has become a good friend as he travelled his own road back to confidence. Psychologist Christine Webber, who has given me some wonderful advice in the past, has also come on board to pass on her wise words and professional advice.

This book is about empowerment. It's about finding the courage to live the life you want, *your* way. My dream is for every one of you who reads this book to become happier and to feel good about yourself, so that, before you know it, you will be radiating strong, inner confidence for all to see.

I want you to think of this book as your own personal toolkit for building and increasing your confidence. A toolkit filled with information, advice, tips, stories and surprises that, together, add up to the secret of real, deep-down confidence. Keep it with you, dip in and out of it, choose sections that feel helpful or illuminating depending on the situation you're in. I truly hope that *Confidence: The Secret* will become like an old friend you can return to time and time again. Because, with the right tools and a bit of determination, we can all do amazing things.

CHAPTER 1

What is Confidence?

I think we've all got a pretty good idea of what confidence is: it's when you feel self-assured, on top of your game, when you know what you're doing and know that you can do it well. Isn't it?

Well, for me, there's so much more to it than that. For a start, confidence can vary enormously, depending on the situation we're in, the way we feel about ourselves on any particular day and what's happening in our lives at that time.

I've met women who are confident about running a company but who tell me they have no confidence at all when it comes to how they dress. I know adults who seem really sociable one-on-one but who confess they are painfully shy at parties. And I've also met plenty of people who seem more than capable running their own lives but who say that they become frozen with panic at the prospect of looking after a small child.

We're none of us perfect, and none of us feel equally confident in every part of our lives. But when you dig a little deeper you can see that those people who exude genuine confidence all have something in common: they believe that they are worthwhile, they value themselves and feel good about themselves – no matter what situation they are in.

That's the kind of confidence we all deserve to have.

Self-Esteem

For me, real confidence stems from self-esteem. A lot of people think that confidence is the same thing as self-esteem, but conversations I've had with therapists and psychologists have convinced me that it's not.

Confidence is our belief in our own abilities – in other words, whether we expect to be good at something and able to cope or not. But self-esteem is how you regard and rate yourself overall. It's not about specific situations, it's about the way you see yourself.

'Esteem' comes from 'estimate'. Self-esteem is your estimation of your own value. High self-esteem means feeling that you are essentially worthwhile and valuable, no matter whether you're good at something or haven't a clue. It doesn't mean that you always know what you are doing, or that things always go right, but it means that when they go wrong you don't feel bad about yourself, or blame yourself out of all proportion.

So, what difference does it make to your confidence if you have low self-esteem? The answer is, a lot.

The reason for this is that people who have low self-esteem, and who therefore estimate or rate themselves in a very negative way, usually believe detrimental and untrue things about themselves. These might include thinking that they are:

- Unlovable
- Unlikable
- Stupid
- Hopeless
- No good at anything.

When men or women have these sorts of beliefs, life is usually very tough for them. They are condemning their *whole* selves, giving themselves a very low rating, and this makes building their own confidence extraordinarily difficult.

So where does self-esteem come from? Why is it that some people seem calmly comfortable in their own skin while the rest of us run around like headless chickens the moment we're asked to do something that takes us beyond what feels safe, comfortable and easy?

The roots of how we feel about ourselves lie in childhood. As children our self-esteem, self-confidence and self-respect can be nurtured or undermined by the adults around us. If we are respected, loved, valued and encouraged to trust ourselves, then our self-esteem will be high.

Looking at my own life, I think I grew up with healthy self-esteem, and I'm sure that was because my family gave me a lot of love and I knew I could rely on them for huge amounts of support and affection. Although I didn't see it at the time, when the worst happened and I nearly died, the fact that I had always viewed myself in a positive way really helped in my recovery.

Although the adults around us – parents, teachers and anyone else who is a part of our life – have a lot of influence, our self-esteem is not only down to how they treated us; our own choices and decisions, even when we're young, also play a part in building up, or knocking down, our self-esteem. And, of course, once we're adults, the way we feel about ourselves is entirely up to us. No matter how difficult life can seem at times, blaming others for the way we feel about ourselves is never going to help. We have choices to make about our lives, our decisions and how we view ourselves. Just as no one else can breathe for us, no one else can give us the ability to trust or to love and care for ourselves.

So, it's up to us. And the good news is that self-esteem, which is all about self-trust and self-love, isn't fixed; it isn't set in stone and unchangeable after a certain age or stage in our life. We can affect and alter it, raise or lower it. So if you feel your self-esteem is low, make it your goal to boost it, starting today, with every choice and decision you make.

From the inside out

A mistake so many of us make is to look for self-esteem outside ourselves. We crave praise, affection, affirmation and admiration from others. Who doesn't enjoy those things? But lovely as those compliments are when they come our way, they can never make us feel better about ourselves for more than a brief moment. If your self-esteem is low, the glow soon wears off. And in just the same way, unkindness and criticism shouldn't affect the way we feel about ourselves more than briefly. Those things hurt, but if you have high-self esteem that pain soon passes and, at your core, you will still feel valuable and worthwhile.

High self-esteem, a positive view of ourselves, has to come from inside. It doesn't come from something someone says or from an event or occurrence – such as getting the job you wanted or falling in love – it comes from within yourself and it has to be a conscious choice. You can choose to do and think the things that will raise your self-esteem, or you can do the opposite and feel worse about yourself.

So what is it we need to do, or think, in order to have a higher level of self-esteem? Well, there are certain behaviours that by their nature make us feel good about ourselves. And by good I don't mean smug or self-congratulatory, I mean that they give us a genuine sense of worth.

Here are some examples:

- Doing what we've said we will do
- Being truthful
- Being kind, generous and appreciative to those around us
- Choosing not to judge others
- Listening to others, especially those closest to us
- Fulfilling our abilities – in work, creatively, or in any other way
- Sticking to our boundaries – saying no when we need to.

This last one is so important. Most of us want to please others, to be liked and to win approval, so the temptation is to keep saying yes, even when it takes a real toll on us. It can be incredibly difficult to say no, and yet the act of saying no can in fact be very empowering.

I don't mean an angry 'no', or an 'I'm at my limit, don't ask me for one more thing' kind of 'no'. What I mean by no is a simple, polite, but firm 'no'. This kind of refusal seldom offends, and it leaves everyone – including you – knowing exactly where they stand.

I used to be a yes girl through and through, always ready to help out or take on an extra task. Learning to say no was an important step in my confidence journey. A few years ago, as the Foundation grew and I was busy opening letters, raising funds, giving talks, mentoring new members and attending meetings, I found myself saying yes to everything. I went to every event and tried to be everything I thought people wanted me to be. I was scared to offend or upset people or embarrass them by turning them down. But I was saving nothing at all for me, and in the end I became exhausted and wrung out.

While I was excited that the Foundation was growing, and I wanted to do everything I could to raise awareness and help others, I was still undergoing regular operations and spending time in recovery myself. And it was all too much. Without meaning to, I started relying on alcohol to numb the exhaustion and get me through the days. And, of course, it didn't help at all – it never does.

It took a wise counsellor to remind me, 'It's OK to not be everything everyone wants you to be'.

It was a revelation. I'd found myself put on a pedestal, labelled inspirational, brave, a success, and it was a huge pressure. I was telling myself, 'I've got to be all those things all the time'. That was not possible, of course, but I did my best to live up to what I thought was expected of me. I didn't feel inspirational or brave; I just felt I was doing what I could and what I believed in, but most of the time I was only just about coping. I also felt like I'd lost the right to not cope.

At night, after a 12- or 14-hour day at work, I'd go back to my flat feeling totally worn out. I was living alone, with no one to talk to about all the demands of my day, all my plans, worries, fears and doubts. With nobody to offload to, instead I'd have a 'comforting' glass of wine.

I knew I needed to find a better way to handle the pressure. Especially when a friend said, 'Wow, you drink a lot'.

So, after talking to the counsellor I started to say no. It's not easy – a bit like trying to flex a withered muscle. You have to build it up, bit by bit. But after a while I began to find it easier to say, 'Sorry, I can't do that, I'm not up to it, I can't fulfil that role, I can't fit that in.' I still wanted to be as helpful as possible, so when I could I'd say, 'I can't do it, but I know someone who can.' And as I began to say no more often, I also began to learn that sometimes, when you say no to others, you say yes to yourself.

Say Yes to You

We've, most of us, grown up believing that it's wrong to be selfish. It's better to put others first, to ignore our own wants. And there's truth in this: generosity and concern for others matters a lot. But to be 'selfish' can sometimes be the right thing, especially when it means caring for yourself, nurturing yourself, knowing your own limits and making sure that you don't burn out, become ill or reach for one too many drinks. If you don't look after your own self-interests, then no one can do it for you.

Sometimes it's only when you're ill, exhausted or about to

explode that you realise you've been running on empty for a while, without putting anything back in the tank.

To look after yourself properly, to feel able to say no when you need to, you have to know yourself. You have to be able to ask yourself, what is it that I need right now? That may sound simple, but actually, when you're caught up in the whirlwind of life, it can be easy to lose track of what you need. And if you don't check in with yourself regularly, not knowing what you need, and as a result not meeting your needs, can become a habit.

What you need might be as simple as five minutes to yourself with a cup of tea, an hour at the gym, an early night, or a laugh with a friend. Only you can know. And only you can say yes to yourself.

It can be even harder with children around. They want you, need you, make demands on you, depend on you and – most of the time – delight you. It can be terribly easy to keep saying yes. But the occasional no is good for your kids and good for you.

As the Foundation grew and my role became more public, I had to learn to say no to some of the requests I was receiving, and instead to say yes to a bit more 'me' time. The difference it made was fantastic. I started to think more about which things I *wanted* to do, about which things would have the most impact, and which ones I could in good conscience say no to. And as I did, I got to know myself better, I felt stronger, braver and happier. The funny thing is, no one seemed to mind me saying no. Much to my amazement, the world didn't fall apart! In fact, I'm assured by those closest to me, I became a little more relaxed, available for the fun stuff in life and a bit less uptight. Really? Me, uptight?

I have to laugh here, because I know I can be a bit of a perfectionist, a bit on the bossy side. I am prone to anxiety and can suddenly decide to clean the entire kitchen at midnight if there's something on my mind. But learning to set some healthy boundaries has been so good for me – it's given me more choices and a stronger sense of what matters most and what I really want to be doing with my time. It's helped me to live more consciously, and by that I mean rather than going through life with blinkers on, refusing to acknowledge how I felt and what I wanted and needed, I started to become more aware of myself and of those around me. I asked myself how I was feeling a bit more often, and then, if I was feeling overwhelmed, tired or worried, I thought about what might help pick me up – and acted on it.

Becoming more self-aware is vital if you are going to raise your self-esteem. Stopping to take a look at what we do, why we do it and what needs to change is a great habit to cultivate, and it's the key to change. Not just to learning to say no, but to deciding what – and who – matters most, what you want out of life and what you are prepared to do to achieve it.

Throughout this book I'll be coming back to the concept of self-esteem and how high self-esteem leads to greater levels of confidence in all areas of life. Because the biggest secret of all about confidence is – anyone can have it. It isn't related to how attractive you are, your age, your job, whether or not you're in a relationship, your friends, or your children. It's simply about who you are inside and how you feel about yourself.

Fighting Spirit

I had been a conventionally pretty girl, but I'd taken my looks for granted. After my attack, my face had to be rebuilt, bit by bit, in operation after operation, using skin grafts from other parts of my body. I lost my eyelids, my nose and lips, and all of the skin on my face and chest. I didn't dare to look in a mirror for a very long time, and when I finally did I saw someone else, not the Katie I had known before.

The surgeons, in particular chief surgeon Mr Jawad, worked with such care, dedication and expertise. But they couldn't give me back my old face. All they could do was create a new face for me, one that is a testament to their skill and to what I have been through, but which is inevitably different.

People sometimes tell me they're in awe that I can still be confident, after all that I've been through. But on the inside, I'm still me. I may look different, and I've been through a lot, but I'm still the same person at heart – the same outgoing woman who loves glamorous clothes, stylish make-up, fun concerts and nights out, new challenges and old friends. I strongly believe that someone can't take from you what they can't see and touch. So although my body was damaged by that cup of acid, my spirit was not, and it's my fighting spirit that has got me through and that gets me onto my feet each time I stand up in front of an audience or a television camera.

Of course, it didn't happen overnight. When I first agreed to let Channel 4 make a documentary about what happened to me, it was because I felt I had nothing left to lose. They warned me that it might not work out and they might never even show it, and I thought that if they did eventually show it probably only a handful of people would actually watch it. So it wasn't really a brave thing to do, it was more a case of thinking 'why not?' I figured, let's just see what happens.

The documentary, *My Beautiful Face*, was a success beyond anything I had imagined. After it was broadcast, hundreds of people got in touch with me, many of them to tell me that they had also been burned, or injured, and that they too had felt like they were the only one going through something like this.

And that's how the Katie Piper Foundation was born. At the time, there was no organisation offering help for people needing to access burns rehabilitation. In the early days of my recovery, when I fearfully wondered whether, at 24, my life might as well be over, I used to desperately search the internet for something – or someone – who could help me, or who was dealing with the same sort of thing. I'd write ridiculous things in the search bar, like 'help me, I'm burned', or 'how to meet men who don't mind if you are disfigured' or 'how to put make-up on a burned face'. But it didn't matter what I searched for, there was nothing out there, apart from a few American web forums on which people would compare their injuries and argue over who was worse off or most unhappy. Hardly cheering stuff.

I couldn't find anything that encouraged me to think I could lead a normal life. If you survive an accident or some kind of life-threatening event, it seems you're expected to be happy just to be alive, never mind hoping for more. I could find no evidence online – or indeed anywhere else – of burns survivors who were out there living their lives in any way that was approaching normal, let alone aspirational. It didn't seem possible for a burned, partially sighted, disabled woman to retrain, study, find a good job, be considered attractive or ever get married and have a family.

Even after the documentary had aired, when I was becoming better known, journalists would ask me questions like, 'How will you ever work?' 'Will you always be dependent on other people?' and even 'Do you think you will ever get married?'

Thank goodness for my fighting spirit. That was what kept me thinking, 'Well, why *wouldn't* I work? Why *couldn't* I live on my own? *Why* can't I have a relationship?' It's what eventually spurred me to do something not just for myself but also for other people like me, for those floundering out there alone after a life-changing event had knocked them off course, too.

I had to dig deep to find the confidence to start the Foundation, but in a funny kind of way, I felt I had no choice. There had been no organisation that I could relate to, so how could I not try to provide help for others in the same predicament?

At first there was only me and the big piles of letters, which I went through one by one myself. I started out with no funds, so I had to find donors, asking them to give their support, money and advice. And when I was asked to come and talk to different organisations and groups, I had to stand up in front of them and speak.

The first time I was asked to give a talk I told myself I was crazy to have accepted. What was I thinking? Looking out at a roomful of expectant faces – all waiting for me to say something interesting, funny or wise – was so daunting, but somehow I did it, though I'm not sure I remembered to breathe at the same time! When I finished speaking, there was an excruciating moment of silence. I wasn't sure how it had gone, until the applause began, and I looked around at a sea of smiling faces and people on their feet. It was a fantastic feeling, and a great confidence boost. So I did it again, and again, and I quickly found that the talks I was giving were not just helping drum up support for the charity but were also helping other people find strength and courage to deal with the problems in their own lives. Not necessarily those with burns or injuries, but people with all kinds of challenges, issues, doubts and fears. In those talks I told the story of how, after what happened to me, I took back control of my life and turned it around, and by sharing my experiences with audiences I discovered I was giving encouragement to others. People told me I was brave, but I thought, well, sometimes being brave is the only choice you have.

These days, I love giving talks: it boosts my spirits to be reminded of the journey I've been on and the challenges I've overcome. I still get butterflies each time before I start, but I know now that people want to hear what I have to say, that they're interested and supportive. And I'm not telling a story about something horrendous that happened, with nothing but gory details and negativity, I'm telling a story about keeping hope alive, of success and achievement despite how hard it was, and of how I was able to move forward and reclaim my future.

I often open my talks with a line borrowed from a political speech given by Gordon Brown on International Women's Day: 'You can survive without food for three weeks; you can survive without water for three days and without air for three minutes; but you cannot survive without hope.'

It's a powerful message, and one that holds true. When you feel lost in the dark, in pain, afraid and with no clear way forward, it's hope that carries and sustains you. We are, all of us, lucky enough to have the capacity for hope, and that is what propels us through the most difficult of times.

The incredibly hard work involved in establishing and building

... helped me regain much of my confidence. It gave ... ng concrete to focus on, to work for and to strive to ... nd so I became focused and determined. I spent a great ... time making sure I was as informed as I could possibly be about all the business details, and I quickly found myself becoming more assertive, enough that I was soon able to chair a board meeting. But even though I now felt confident and composed in the boardroom, in my personal life I couldn't begin to summon up the confidence to speak to a guy in a bar. The very idea of it made me feel self-conscious and tongue-tied, and I was so afraid of rejection that I seldom tried to meet any new people socially, let alone go on a date. It was a long haul from there to eventually meeting the man I married – a story you may know from my previous books and which I'll go into again later in this book – but what I did realise even then, in the miserable aftermath of wrong choices and being stood up by the wrong men, was that I couldn't – I *wouldn't* – give up and let another person's actions dictate my future.

Choose Your Future

I always say that what happens to you is only ten per cent of the story; the other ninety per cent is what happens afterwards.

No one illustrates this better than beauty blogger Jordan Bone. Jordan is gutsy, bright and beautiful, and she's proving, day after day, that nothing can hold you back if you refuse to let it.

Jordan could have settled for feeling eternally sorry for herself. In 2005, when she was only 15, she accepted a lift in a car driven by a boy of 17. The car crashed. Jordan was in the back, and of the four teenagers in the car, she was the most seriously injured. After six months in a spinal injuries unit, she finally went home in a wheelchair, paralysed from the chest down and with extremely limited movement in her hands.

All Jordan's hopes and dreams seemed to be over. She now needed help with everything, which meant no privacy or independence, and she struggled to see a future for herself.

'I was on antidepressants,' Jordan says. 'I really felt my life was over. But one of the things I still had was the internet. One day I discovered a guided meditation video on YouTube and I thought, why not? I kept going back to it every day and I began to feel so much happier. I got a webcam and decided to make some videos, just for myself, really, I never expected anyone to look at them. But to my surprise a handful of people did watch them and a couple of them said, "I like your make-up". That sparked an idea – why not post make-up videos? I'd always loved make-up.

'My biggest challenge was teaching myself how to put it on, because I can't control my fingers. But I taught myself a way of holding the brushes using my hands and mouth, and although at first it was a disaster, I practised over and over again until I could do it.'

Jordan's YouTube channel and the blog that followed ('Jordan's Beautiful Life') now have many thousands of followers, including Kylie Jenner, one of the famed Kardashian family and daughter of Kris and Caitlyn (formerly Bruce) Jenner.

When I came across Jordan's blog and videos, I was amazed by her skill with make-up and loved her ideas. I learned such a lot by watching her. Like many of her viewers, I had no clue how challenging it was for her to put on her make-up, until she posted a very personal and moving video titled 'My Beautiful Struggle', in which she showed us just what it takes for her to appear so glamorous and perfectly made-up.

Jordan was my special guest at the Ideal Home Show Diversity Catwalk and I was delighted that she could come along and talk about her blog and all that she's achieved.

At 26, Jordan is now engaged, she and her fiancé Michael are building a house, she goes to the gym, runs her blog and video channel and also finds time to campaign for road safety, giving moving talks to groups of teenagers.

Jordan hasn't let anything stop her from having a successful life. She has an army of followers and is regularly invited to take part in high-profile cosmetic industry events. Thanks to her blog and bravery, she helps set trends and influences thousands of young girls.

Jordan is somebody who – based on society's unwritten rules – should have absolutely no confidence. But she's been able to find the secret that so many people are searching for. She is brimming with confidence, has a gorgeous and infectious smile, and when people watch her videos the last thing they think about is the fact that she's in a wheelchair.

'We've only got one life,' she says. 'You've got to live it and believe in yourself. So if something is standing in your way, maybe it means you just need to try a different way.'

Exactly.

I truly hope that, on your path to greater confidence, you will learn to harness your fighting spirit, actively choose behaviours that boost your confidence, and begin to say 'no' to some of life's demands and a great big 'yes' to yourself.

Tips for Building Your Self-Esteem

These are things you can do every day to make yourself feel lighter, happier, more attractive and more deserving of the good things in life.

- Laugh! Tell a joke, or listen to one, share a funny anecdote or do something that you know will make you laugh – instant happiness boost!
- Appreciate three things about yourself. Your looks, health, a particular ability, something good you did today, someone you helped, listened to or advised – there's a long list of possibilities, believe me. Write them down and keep them – soon you'll have a lot of them to look through for a pick-me-up whenever you feel down.
- Do something kind for someone else. Buy a colleague a coffee, help a stranger, leave a generous tip in a restaurant, pay someone a compliment or simply smile at someone.
- If someone or something makes you feel uncomfortable, listen to yourself and walk away – or switch off.
- Put a little bit of 'me' time into each day and use it to do something you enjoy.
- Do something different – walk instead of taking the bus, play with your children instead of working when you get home, cook a new dish, have a go at meditation, or watch a TED talk and feel inspired.

CHAPTER

2

The Not-Good-Enough Tape

Of all the ways by which we damage our self-esteem and diminish our confidence, being overly self-critical is the worst. The way you feel about yourself and how highly you value yourself depends on how you think about and talk to yourself. So if you are constantly thinking critical things about yourself, it follows that you're not going to feel especially good.

Repetitive harsh and critical thoughts will affect most aspects of your life, squeezing the joy, fun and spontaneity out of you. So if there's a tape on a loop in your head saying 'not good enough', it's time to change the tape. It can be done, no matter how long that tape has been running, and I'm going to show you how.

Once that tape has been changed, you'll find that one of the biggest roadblocks to confidence, and peace of mind, has been cleared away, and you'll wonder why you didn't press the mute button sooner!

Choosing Your Response

If you've read any of my earlier books, you'll know that I've learned a lot from having CBT (cognitive behavioural therapy), and I'd like to pass on some of that to you.

Although all sorts of bad things can happen to us, it's our own personal *response* to those things that determines how we feel about them and therefore what we decide to do next.

Let me give you an example.

Suppose you're feeling low, so you ring a friend for a chat. Unfortunately, instead of settling down at the other end for a natter, she says: 'Sorry, can't speak right now. Something's come up.'

How will you feel about that? Perhaps you'll feel more miserable than you did before you picked up the phone. But has your friend caused this unhappiness? No, she hasn't. It's your response to what she's said that has caused the problem because, almost certainly, you've lapsed into a spiral of unhelpful thinking which has in turn made your mood plummet.

For example, you might think:

- She's probably got more interesting people to talk to.
- She must think I'm a drag.
- Perhaps she doesn't like me any more.
- I bet she wants to end our friendship.

If you're thinking negative things like that, you're guaranteed to be inconsolable in no time! And these nagging thoughts – known as inner commentary (more on this shortly) – are largely responsible for your misery.

In reality, there may be all sorts of reasons why your friend had no time to talk.

For instance:

- She could have been in the middle of a row with her husband.
- She might have been helping her kids with some difficult homework.
- She could have been running late for an appointment.
- She might have had visitors.

Unfortunately, when we lack confidence or feel low, we often don't stop to consider alternatives, we just jump to negative conclusions that make us feel even worse. While you might be convincing yourself that your friend doesn't even want to know you, actually she might be feeling sorry that she couldn't enjoy a chat.

So next time a situation like this happens to you, ask yourself if there is any hard evidence for what you are thinking. Often there isn't! Ask yourself if there might be an alternative explanation. Frequently, there is.

Once you have realised – and accepted – that your own thoughts and beliefs can make difficult situations worse, something that can be a real help is to make a list of the kind of negative thoughts, or inner commentary, that tend to pop into your head.

We all have an inner commentary. We have NICs (Negative Inner Commentaries) and if we're lucky we also have some PICs (Positive Inner Commentaries). What I want to do is to help you replace some of your NICs with PICs.

NICs have usually been in our heads for a very long time,

because many of them stem from things people said to us in our childhood.

Common ones are:

- I'm hopeless at most things.
- I'm a mess.
- I'm not as good at things as other people.
- People don't like me.
- I'm stupid.
- I'm unlovable.
- I'm different from most people.
- Other people have more friends.
- I'm not interesting.

These NICs are not true, but the trouble is, because when they were first said to us we believed them, they've continued buzzing around in our heads for years as 'truths' without us ever pausing to examine whether they *ought* to be there.

An accountant friend of mine, let's call her Annie, once told me how, deep down, she had always believed herself to be 'thick'. And because of that, she had NICs that said:

- I'm not as clever as other people.
- I'll never make much money.
- I'm not as good at being an accountant as others I trained with.

With these beliefs running through her head on a loop, Annie remained in a small company, keeping a low profile and never putting herself forward for promotion or a more interesting job. Even though she was bored and under-used, she thought she was lucky to have any job at all.

Eventually, miserable with her life, Annie went to see a counsellor, who challenged these NICs that Annie had and asked her to consider where they had first come from.

Annie realised that she could trace them back to a time when, as a young teenager, she had been constantly criticised and ridiculed by a teacher who was forever saying to her: 'If you can't understand that, you must be stupid,' and 'You'll never amount to anything.'

Annie started thinking about the teacher who had been so unkind and quick to dismiss her abilities. She still knew several people from her home town who had also been taught by this particular woman, so she asked them what they could remember about her. Everyone recalled her in a very negative way. Some of the comments were:

- She was completely dysfunctional.
- She was hopeless at explaining things.
- She was cruel; I'm a teacher and I would never speak to kids like that.
- Looking back, I'm convinced she wasn't very bright.
- She only got on with cats – and couldn't stand humans!

Annie suddenly realised that she had spent years believing the opinion of this teacher when actually the teacher was not someone whose opinion she *should* value.

'After all,' Annie said, 'would I like this teacher if I met her now? Probably not! Looking back, do I think this teacher explained things well? No. Was the teacher someone who was kind and supportive and thought carefully about what she was saying to impressionable young pupils? Definitely not. I believed what she told me because I was young and she was in a position of authority, but I'm not a child any longer and I don't need to hang on to the messages she gave me.'

What Annie did next was to look for some evidence in her life that she *was* intelligent. She spoke to family, friends and colleagues, who gave her a lot of very positive feedback. 'You're one of the brightest people I know,' one friend told her. 'I always knew you were clever,' her mother said. And her co-worker told her, 'You could get a much better job if you wanted, I often wonder why you've stayed here so long.'

With her counsellor's support, Annie began to replace the tired old negative messages with positive ones.

- I am clever and intelligent.
- I am a good accountant.
- I can handle challenges.
- I deserve a great job.

Six months later she got that dream job, and she hasn't looked back. 'I was halfway through my thirties before the penny dropped,' she told me. 'But look at me now: I love my new job and I feel good about my abilities and so much more confident.'

The lesson here, for all of us, is to look hard at the messages we're giving ourselves, then to question the negative ones and take steps to replace them with positive ones. It requires time, effort and practice, but stick at it and it really does work.

Bear in mind that if you are severely lacking in confidence you can't suddenly turn an NIC such as 'I'm hopeless' into a PIC which says 'I am great at everything'. That would be too big a leap. So break it down into smaller pieces. 'I am hopeless at making new friends' can first become 'I like to make new friends' and eventually 'I make new friends easily'. If you say it often enough, you will start to believe it and act on it.

It may not happen overnight, but this is something that with determination and practice can make a huge difference to the way you feel about yourself. It really does work, because the way we speak to ourselves has so much influence over the way we feel about ourselves. So, even if it feels forced, begin to give yourself some more positive, hopeful and uplifting messages.

Don't Feed the Monster

I have an inner commentary that can be very negative at times. I call it the monster inside me, and I have to be disciplined about catching it and stopping it in its tracks.

Not long after I met my husband, Richard James (Richie), he suggested I come to his home to meet his family. I was so worried. What on earth would they think of me? Would they compare me to his previous girlfriend? Would they think I was wrong for him, or be concerned that my health problems would make me too high-maintenance? The more I worried about it, the more insecure I became.

Then I realised what I was doing to myself – I was creating a problem where there wasn't one, and might never be one, and I was giving myself a hard time about things I couldn't change.

I remembered an exercise a psychologist had once taught me. I sat down with a piece of paper and a pen and wrote out all the things I could offer to enrich Richie's life and our relationship.

I thought of one thing, and then stopped. Er, was there anything else? Then it began to flow.

For example:

- I had travelled to a lot to different countries he hadn't been to, so I could tell him interesting things about other places and cultures.
- I knew the best places to eat in London, and he had never lived there or tried them.
- I had experienced tough times, so I knew about patience, determination and perseverance.
- I was good in a crisis – whether that was a burst pipe or a medical emergency.
- I loved to have fun, to laugh and enjoy life.

By the time I'd finished, I had quite a substantial list and I felt so much better.

This is a great exercise which I highly recommend – whether you're nervous about meeting your boyfriend's family, a job interview or going to a party, remember all the positive things you have to offer that others will appreciate.

The monster inside me can affect my professional life, too. It sometimes wakes up unexpectedly and starts to attack. After giving a talk, I might find myself thinking, 'The audience didn't give me as warm a reception this week as they did last week – am I losing my touch? Or, 'That episode of *Bodyshockers* didn't achieve the same viewing figures as the previous episode, should I really be doing this?' But then I think, 'Hang on a minute, this is just the monster inside you. Are you going to let it dominate and destroy everything you've worked for?'

Sometimes I can silence the monster inside by simply faking confidence. I did it when I appeared on Radio 4's *Woman's Hour* recently. I was invited to talk about appearance and invisibility, and I felt daunted by the experts – a philosopher and a well-known political commentator – who were appearing on the show alongside me.

Next to them, I felt like a bit of a fraud, and very out of my depth, but on the way there I realised that if I went in and said, 'Hi, I'm Katie, I don't know why they've chosen me, I know nothing about this, I shouldn't really be here at all,' which is what I was thinking, then I would be putting myself down and they would probably agree that I didn't belong there. So instead I took a deep breath, went in, stood tall and acted as if I was confident, making sure I spoke slowly and clearly.

I knew that whatever I showed on the surface was what everyone else would believe, and that's how they would view me. So I spoke about what I knew, my area, and it was fine. I realised that I was an expert, too, in my own field.

Giving myself a little pep talk can work wonders. It calms the monster and reminds me that I do have a lot to offer. I believe that the mind is the strongest muscle we have, the power it has can be incredible. We really can choose our outcome. The scientists among you, or those who paid attention at school, might know Newton's third law – for every action there is an equal and opposite reaction. Newton was talking about physics and the physical world around us, but I think his law is true for our inner worlds, too. If we put out negative beliefs about ourselves, that's what we'll get reflected back at us.

Feeding the monster inside is like feeding trolls who post unkind comments on social media, it just gives them power. Trolls, those people who post cruel and nasty criticisms online, aren't people we respect, or people whose opinions truly matter to us. And the monster is the same: give it too much time and attention and it grows. It's far better to starve it by refusing to think negative thoughts, and then to shrink it with a stream of positive ones.

Don't keep feeding the monster. I always remind myself that the monster's only there if I feed it.

Here's a useful tip: when the monster starts to surface, and those self-critical thoughts start to buzz through your mind, have a 'stop word' ready. It could be anything – banana, giggle, ice cream. I find something daft works best. As soon as a negative thought surfaces, think of your chosen stop word – even say it out loud if you want – and catch that negative thought in its tracks. Then consciously turn to something more positive.

Affirmations

I'm a great fan of Louise Hay, a remarkable woman in her nineties who is the author of several bestselling self-help books and the founder of a charity as well as her own publishing house. After a tough childhood, Louise left school without qualifications and worked in low-paid jobs. But she went on to discover, through a series of events, the power of positive thinking and forgiveness. She became the queen of positive affirmations – she's published various compilation books of them – and with their help she turned her life around, built herself an amazing career, and has had a beneficial impact on countless other people's lives.

What I like about Louise's approach is that it's so simple. She points out that when we engage with a negative message, such as a worry or a fear, we repeat it to ourselves over and over again, drumming it into our consciousness. If you're worried about a bill, for instance, you might think, 'How am I going to pay that bill?' several hundred times a day. So to counteract that you need to choose a positive affirmation and repeat it to yourself as often as you can. In that instance you might choose, 'I pay my bills with ease and joy'. It might feel weird at first, but the idea is to change your mind-set and allow yourself to believe that you *can* find solutions to problems and take charge of your life.

In the early days of my recovery I found this approach a great help. When no one believed I would ever be anything but an invalid, positive thinkers like Louise and Rhonda Byrne (author of *The Secret*) gave me the encouragement I needed to believe that maybe there was a future for me. I listened to *The Secret* – which is all about positive thought – as an audiobook and practised simple affirmations day after day, at a time when I couldn't yet go outside the house, let alone imagine a career and a family.

Louise suggests you take a simple affirmation such as 'I love and approve of myself' and just keep repeating it, until it becomes second nature. At first it can feel unnatural, but it's a challenge worth pushing through, because it really does have a powerful effect. And, essentially, you're training yourself to see your life and your potential differently.

The Power of Exercise

One thing that I believe helps a lot with silencing our inner critic and turning those Negative Inner Commentaries into positive ones is physical exercise. It's amazing how simply moving your body and getting your blood pumping can help to change the way you treat and talk to yourself.

Most of us focus pretty heavily on how we look – our self-image is tied up with what we see in the mirror each day. Studies have shown that when we exercise it gets us thinking about what our bodies can *do*, rather than what they look like. Instead of slumping on the sofa thinking, 'I hate my legs', make yourself get up and move, while consciously shifting your thoughts to something like, 'My legs are strong: they allow me to run/take a dance class/go to the gym.' Taking time to appreciate what your body can do really helps you to shut down negative thoughts and begin seeing yourself differently.

This approach definitely worked for me. I started doing lots of exercise during my recovery, once I'd discovered it could help me ward off depression and create a sense of discipline in my life at a time when it was still very unstructured and most things felt out of my control. Before I was attacked, I used to go to the gym sometimes, but it was mainly to help me stay slim. Back then I drank and smoked and didn't think much about my health. After the attack, I started running and I've since done five- and ten-kilometre runs, charity runs and even a few half-marathons. When I set up the Foundation and we opened an office, I would run there each morning, and I would also run to the Channel 4 studios on the days when I was working with them. I'd have a quick wash in the toilets, change into a dress and heels, and I was ready to work. On a practical level, running got me to the places where I needed to be, but I loved that I was benefiting from the physical exercise at the same time.

The difference it made was incredible. When you exercise often, you get stronger, fitter and more supple, and as a result it makes you feel great about yourself and your body. Running also gives you valuable headspace, some quality thinking time with minimal distractions. And believe me, it's very difficult to fixate on negative thoughts while you're pounding along the streets with your legs working hard and your heart beating in your ears. It makes you feel motivated and alive, and it also naturally focuses your mind towards positive things. And the more good and positive thoughts you fill your head with, the less room it leaves for negative ones, even once you've slowed down and stopped running.

If you have a friend who also wants to shift their thought patterns, or who simply fancies getting more active, you could decide to exercise together. Not only does this help motivate you both to stick at it, but it can also have a beneficial effect on your friendship as you help each other work towards your goals.

Kerry Montgomery, another of the models involved in my Ideal Home Show Diversity Catwalk, tells me that she also discovered the power of exercise a few years ago. Kerry, who is 33 and is close to completing her PhD in psychology, was born with a genetic condition called Crouzon Syndrome, which affected the appearance of her face and caused a number of health problems.

'Crouzons can make your face look a bit squashed,' Kerry says. 'The tubes behind your face are not as wide as they are in other people's, so as well as having a number of operations, I suffered a lot from sinusitis, ear and chest infections, colds and breathing difficulties.

'A few years ago, I decided to take up running, in the hope of improving my health. I started small, running just a few hundred yards at a time, but I kept at it until eventually I was able to run a marathon. It felt amazing, and the benefits were unbelievable. My health improved dramatically, and so did my confidence. I hadn't expected that, but it was so good to see what my body was capable of: I lost weight, got into much better shape and felt great about myself. I hadn't set out to lose weight, but I loved what my body could do and it gave me confidence.

'When I was younger, other kids used to make nasty comments and I would feel awful about myself, criticising myself non-stop, not just for my facial difference but for being fat, stupid – anything, really. But the confidence boost that running gave me meant I was no longer bothered when people stared at me or made comments about my face. I just thought, "that's their problem" and ignored it.'

Although Kerry and I both get so much out of running, in fact any form of exercise can have the same effect. So choose whatever sport or physical activity you fancy, whether it's something you've done before or a totally new pastime, and do your best stick at it – not only will you witness yourself get fitter, but you'll help silence that inner critic, too. Result!

Stop Judging

Nobody likes to be judged by others, and yet most of us do it – we look at other people and make instant judgements based on very little background knowledge. All too often these judgements are negative and critical.

If you are frequently critical of yourself, with a strong Negative Inner Commentary running on a loop most of the time, then chances are you are critical of others, too. That's how it tends to work. Inner criticism leads to outer criticism.

Ask yourself honestly, do you think you come across as critical to other people?

If the answer is yes, the good news is that when you begin to change your inner critical voice, it also helps you stop feeling so critical towards those around you. So start giving yourself positive inner messages and give yourself, and others, a chance.

I've had to put up with a lot of negative judgements from other people, but I've also learned not to assume anything and that not everyone is automatically critical. I used to think that everyone looking at me was judging me. But since I stopped being so tough on myself, and giving myself horrible messages, I have realised that being looked at isn't always a bad thing. Now if someone looks at me in a supermarket, I think maybe they love my hair colour. Or maybe they empathise, because perhaps underneath their clothes they're burned, too, or someone they know or love has suffered burns.

I look at people all the time. I'm interested in others. I keep my eyes open for great clothes, make-up and hair ideas. I might look at someone's smile, or wonder what kind of day they're having. It's natural. I'm not looking at them to make unkind judgements, so why should I assume that's what anyone looking at me is doing? And, frankly, I wouldn't want people to avoid looking at me at all, because that would be even more uncomfortable, both for me and for them.

I look at others with interest but without feeling critical, and I hope they do the same for me. So try not to make negative judgements about others, give them a chance, and that way you give yourself a chance, too.

Model Images

We live in a fast-moving age when Instagram, Twitter, Facebook and other social media sites are a big part of our lives, and we take, send, view, share and like hundreds of images every day.

It's fun to share photos and to look at what others have chosen to share. But it's also a breeding ground for self-criticism and envy. It's so easy to compare yourself – negatively! – to the images you see and are surrounded by every day and to feel discontented with yourself and wish you had what others seem to have. If only I had her glossy hair, or his toned abs, or her shapely bum, or his perfect nose . . . And then we look at our own bodies and see something that seems inferior.

The trouble is, so many of the images we are bombarded with – especially those online and in magazines, of models and celebrities – are in fact Photoshopped or airbrushed. Even models often wish they truly looked the way they do in the photos! Many celebrities carefully control the photos they put out, and won't post a shot of their tired, hungover face, only the ones that make them look hot, and they go to great lengths to make sure the others never get seen.

So it's important to remember that there are images, and then there's real life, and not to make the mistake of comparing yourself to what isn't real.

Even when images haven't been altered, there's still a lot of illusion that goes hand-in-hand with celebrity. When I upload photos to Instagram, I don't Photoshop them; they show me as I am. More often than not, I've got my hair styled and make-up on, but other than that, it's just me. And you can see very clearly that I'm scarred. Even so, a lot of young girls write comments like, 'She is so beautiful, I wish I looked like her'.

I'm delighted, of course, but I'm aware of the irony. They don't really wish to be disfigured, or to have a face that consists mostly of bits of their back and buttocks repurposed and sewn together. But that isn't what they're seeing when they look at photos of me. They see an image that carries with it a degree of fame and celebrity, an image which to them represents success. They see me as happy, in love, with a gorgeous little daughter; they see me as someone who is on TV and in newspapers and magazines, someone who seems glamorous, with an exciting life. That's what they want, not the disfigurement, and the truth is, they can have it, because anyone can. I'm an ordinary woman, who worked hard to recover my health and to build a career. But there are many routes to becoming a well-known face, and if that's what you want, then go for it!

Not that my life is perfect – of course it isn't. I count my blessings every day, but I still have problems and difficulties like anyone else, not to mention ongoing health issues. And like most other people, there are things about me that I wish were different. You might think my biggest concern would be my scars, but actually I've always wished I was taller. And funnily enough, the diversity models all told me that their specific disability wasn't necessarily what bothered them most about themselves: it was other things – their bum, tum, legs or boobs.

The point is that we all have the shape, height, colouring and features that were handed out at birth. We can choose to make the most of them (and these days there are lots of ways to do that), but there are some things about ourselves that we just can't change. We have to live with them, and learn to love them – because they're part of us. We come as a whole, not a selection of separate body parts, and to me what always matters most is the light in someone's eyes or the warmth in their smile.

It's nice to admire someone, maybe to take a great idea and copy it, but real envy just eats away at you inside. Being envious isn't wrong, since usually you can't help it, but fuelling it with resentment and anger will only leave you feeling stuck and miserable – and full of self-criticism. Instead, channel any envy you feel into something more positive – turn it into a motivational tool that inspires you to become the best you can be.

Challenging our inner critic, swapping our Negative Inner Commentaries for Positive Inner Commentaries, catching ourselves when we start to make judgements, and learning not to judge ourselves: these are ongoing challenges for most of us. But they are challenges worth taking, because the rewards can be huge. You'll feel better about yourself, happier in your own skin and ultimately much more confident.

Happy, positive, life-affirming thoughts allow your confidence to bloom and grow.

Body Confidence

Countless women, and increasingly men, too, lack confidence in their bodies. Whether you think you're too tall or too short, too fat or too thin, or that some aspect of your body is in some way 'wrong', body confidence is a major issue for so many of us. It's a theme I'll come back to repeatedly in this book, because it affects us all so deeply. Even if you're lucky enough to feel good about your body, you probably have a sister, friend, daughter or son who doesn't.

We can't pretend that looks don't matter, because they often do. They've always mattered to some extent, but we live in a time when looks are given more importance than ever before and there's no doubt that feeling comfortable in your own skin and good about the way you look is central to feeling confident. If you feel miserable about your appearance, it's likely to affect all aspects of your life, from work to your social life and relationships.

Learning to like and accept our bodies and our appearance is very much a theme of our time. Social-media sites highlight the endless self-examination, the quest for the perfect body, the comments and criticisms that can build up or undermine our confidence in the way we look.

Going through so much physical change myself has made me very aware of body issues in general. Why is it that so many of us feel unhappy with our appearance? And does making dramatic changes through cosmetic surgery, even if you can afford it and you're brave enough to go through with it, really increase happiness and life satisfaction? This route carries risks and an uncertain outcome; surely there's got to be a better way to feel good about ourselves and the bodies we have than going under the knife?

I believe that it's possible for any of us to develop a more positive and accepting view of our own body. It's great to make the most of what we have, but in the end most people are attracted to someone else not because of their legs, their arms or even their face, but because of their personality, their energy and their warmth. We fall for someone because they are funny or intelligent or interesting, and once we've fallen for them, we honestly don't care whether they have a big bum, or flat feet, chubby knees or a wide forehead.

Step one in developing a more positive attitude to your body is to keep things in perspective and remember that you're not just a collection of body parts, you're a person, with so much going for you beyond what's on the surface.

Nobody's Perfect

I've worked with some gorgeous models, actresses and presenters who seemed pretty perfect to me, but talking to them I discovered that all of them felt they had physical flaws. They believed their legs were too short, or their nose was unattractive, or they disliked a crooked tooth. And I've lost count of how many believed that their bottoms were too big!

When we see images of celebrities and models – and especially if we're lacking in confidence – we tend to believe they're out of our league and completely unlike us. But we forget, as I've already said, that the images we see have usually been manipulated and airbrushed so that the celebrities seem even more 'perfect' than they already are.

The other thing is that many editors and dress designers prefer models to be skeletal, because it's thought that they photograph better and that clothes hang more attractively on them. But most of us will never look the way they do, even if we wanted to. And, more importantly, most of us would never want to go through what they do in order to stay so waif-like.

There has been a steady rise in eating disorders over the past few years, particularly in very young girls, and many experts attribute this to the celebrity culture.

Fortunately, some individuals in the spotlight are beginning to make a stand for common sense. Last year, fashion model Charli Howard, then 23 and with six years of modelling under her belt, publicly criticised her agency on social media for their outrageous demands on her body – and for letting her go because they apparently said she was too big and out of shape. Charli, by the way, is a UK size 6–8 and 5 foot 8 inches tall.

Here's part of what she wrote:

I refuse to feel ashamed and upset on a daily basis for not meeting your ridiculous, unobtainable beauty standards, whilst you sit at a desk all day, shovelling cakes and biscuits down your throats and slagging me and my friends off about our appearance. The more you force us to lose weight and be small, the more designers have to make clothes to fit our sizes, and the more young girls are being made ill. It's no longer an image I choose to represent.

'In case you hadn't realised, I am a woman. I am human. I cannot miraculously shave my hip bones down, just to fit into a sample-size piece of clothing or to meet "agency standards". I have fought nature for a long time, because you've deemed my body shape too "curvaceous", but I have recently begun to love my shape.

Charli's open letter went viral and a lot of people came forward to support her stance. Another positive move last year was that the French passed a law requiring all models working in France to have a medical certificate declaring them fit and well. The hope is that this will outlaw the use of women who are so thin that they become ill.

Perhaps, finally, attitudes about thinness and bodily perfection are beginning to change, but there's still a long way to go. Many people are fed up with seeing models who don't reflect the real world, and there's a powerful movement in favour of realistically-sized women, plus-sized women and women who don't fit the conventional beauty mould. Our Diversity Catwalk at the Ideal Home Show was just a small part of this ongoing campaign.

Do your bit by refusing to be brainwashed by media images. We all know that most women aren't pin-thin – and that's a good thing! Apart from anything else, most men don't fancy someone who's uber-thin, they fancy women with flesh and curves and substance.

My Body Confidence Story

In terms of how I've felt about my body over the course of my life, I've been through three distinct stages: before the attack, immediately afterwards, and then up to the present day. That's very different to most people, whose attitude gradually evolves as they grow older. For me, the changes were sudden and I had to make huge adjustments, but because of that I've known and experienced a whole spectrum of different attitudes towards myself.

Stage One

As a teenager, I felt pretty good about my body. I was a very physical person; I always enjoyed sports and exercise, but I took my health for granted and didn't think about it beyond wanting to be fit and slim. Between the ages of 19 and 23, once I'd left home and moved to London, although I had trained as a beautician I had hoped to become a model and TV presenter. So I really wanted to look good, and I became more conscious of my body shape and size, and of wanting to fit into particular clothes. I was quite confident, but I was trying to make my way in the really competitive and saturated world of modelling (not catwalk, as I wasn't tall enough, but promotional and editorial modelling) and presenting. It was a world in which there was a lot of inherent criticism and self-criticism, and with all that pressure upon me it was almost impossible not to develop a few insecurities.

I didn't see it that way at the time, but it was a shallow world, focused mostly on what was on the outside – in other words, on looks. I was still interested in fitness and sport: I ran and went to the gym and I enjoyed both, but my primary goal was to stay slim.

I enjoyed dressing fashionably; I love gorgeous clothes, sexy dresses, heels, jewellery. I've always enjoyed been a glam girl, so putting together a portfolio and going for presenting and modelling jobs was fun. But as an industry and an existence, it was all skin-deep.

Stage Two

After the attack, my reason for being became entirely about staying alive. In the first year there were really raw, dark, difficult times. I was only 24: very young to have to face such huge changes. I underwent hundreds of operations; I was constantly prodded, poked, sliced, stitched and handled by medical staff. My body was covered in scars, not just from the acid burns but also from the grafts needed to take skin for rebuilding the damaged parts. There was hardly a part of me that hadn't undergone some kind of procedure.

At first I wouldn't look at myself. I had to use giant bed-bath wipes as I couldn't shower because so much of my body was recovering from surgery. I didn't touch myself, shave my legs or look properly at my body for a year, probably closer to two. I virtually disassociated myself; it was easier to pretend the body I was in wasn't mine.

During the second year after the attack I underwent a lot of reconstructive surgery. I was only just beginning to accept all the scars I already had when the medics said, 'We are going to reconstruct your eyelids and we need to take skin from somewhere, where would you least mind having new scars?' They gave me the choice of arms, legs or back. I didn't want new scars, but in the end I just told them to take it from anywhere. I realised that my body was just a vessel; the healthy parts were there to help rebuild the missing or damaged parts. I had to surrender and give my body to the doctors.

I couldn't eat; I was fed through a tube in my stomach because I'd swallowed some of the acid and it had damaged my oesophagus. Because of this I lost a lot of weight, so much that my skin appeared silvery and transparent, and my ribs stuck out. I looked like a little boy. And my body started growing excess hair, a condition called lanugo which can happen when you're starving, as the body tries to protect itself by trapping in heat that muscles can no longer provide.

For two years I had to wear a pressure suit for 23 hours a day, to help heal all the scar sites. With all these things going on, I felt I hardly knew my body any more: it had completely changed and wasn't the body I had been familiar with. I had become an organism struggling for survival, and everything about my existence went into that.

When I did finally see myself naked again, a couple of years later, I didn't recognise myself. I was battered and scarred and utterly changed. For months I wore shapeless clothes in dark colours, tracksuits and flat shoes. I wanted to disappear, to blend into the background and hide; I barely left the house and when I did I felt fearful and anxious. I was terrified of people's reactions when they saw me, and physically I was very unsure of myself, I didn't know any longer what I could manage. Even a short walk to the shops was a major hurdle.

Stage Three

As I began to recover, a strange thing happened. I started to appreciate my body in a new and very different way. I realised that it was strong enough to keep me alive. I was amazed by its ability to cope with so much. My body was battered, but not broken. It was able to give some of its parts in order to mend others, and it had the power to heal itself. I came to see how strong the human body is, and began to view my scars as a celebration of still being alive, of getting better, of still having a future to look forward to.

I learned a lot about gratitude and acceptance from my body. Society, or at least some parts of it, might say my scars were ugly and shameful, but to me my body was a miracle. I now felt proud of it, and kept thinking, 'Look what this body did!' I was grateful that I had been fit and healthy before the attack; because of that I survived and, bit by bit, was able to fight my way back to being a functioning person. I promised myself that I would become fit and healthy again. And this time I would truly appreciate what I had.

I began to question how I 'ought' to be dressing. People like me were not visible in everyday life; the media was full of flawless models while disfigured people were expected to stay out of sight. Was I going to accept that? I hated looking frumpy or dowdy, and I missed wearing lovely clothes. Could I buck society's expectations that someone disfigured should hide away? Could I be injured and scarred and yet still wear lovely clothes and feel proud of the way I looked? I was in my twenties; I wanted a life, a job, a relationship. Wasn't I entitled to all of those things?

I had to ask myself if I was strong enough to swim against the tide, to go against the weight of opinion that said if you're not perfect no one wants to see you, and if you're disfigured you've lost the right to dress in sexy, attractive clothes.

People kept telling me I was brave and patting me on the head. It was OK to be brave, to be a good girl, to be touching

43

and sad or sweet. But I felt like a child, I didn't want to be patted or told I was brave. I was a woman approaching 30, I wanted to be sexy. Eventually I decided I was going to buy a really sexy dress. You can't hide in a sexy dress, you get noticed when you walk into a room. I was taking a big risk. But I did it, and the dress was strapless, showing all of my skin graft on my chest and arm, fitted and tight in brilliant white. I discovered that it's possible to feel sexy even when society and the media says you are not supposed to.

The first time someone said, 'You look really hot in that,' I felt embarrassed. It was very strange receiving a compliment like that after considering myself unsexy for so long. But it was great, too; I was being seen as a woman and not simply as a brave girl or a medical miracle.

After that, I started dressing up for everything. I would turn up to hospital appointments (and for a good few years my life mostly revolved around hospital appointments) in glamorous clothes and heels. It might have raised a few eyebrows, but it made me feel just a little bit more feminine and normal – things that I had lost and so badly wanted to regain.

Through my work with the Foundation and with Channel 4 I started to become known not for what had happened to me but for my charity and television work. There were also some defining moments that contributed enormously to a new sense of body confidence for me. One of them was being invited by Marks and Spencer in 2013 to take part in their groundbreaking advertising campaign. There I was, with eleven other women – including actress Helen Mirren, artist Tracey Emin, Olympic boxer Nicola Adams, ballerina Darcey Bussell and singer Ellie Goulding –

modelling M&S clothes in a short film and a series of photos by brilliant photographer Annie Leibovitz.

What felt fantastic was that I wasn't there because I was disabled, but because I was a TV presenter and charity campaigner. The same was true when I took part in London Fashion Week in 2015. I was invited to appear in Naomi Campbell's Fashion for Relief show, walking down the catwalk with a whole line of supermodels and celebrities to highlight the fight against the Ebola virus. Here was I, with my face reconstructed from my buttocks and back and manmade plastics, taking part alongside women like Alesha Dixon, Sarah Ferguson, Pixie Lott and Vivienne Westwood – all because of what I'd achieved. And on both these occasions I got to wear gorgeous, sexy clothes.

I loved knowing that people would look at the clothes I wore for M&S and in the Fashion Week show and think, 'I like that jacket,' or 'What a great dress,' with their focus being on the clothing rather than on me.

Until recently there has been no real platform for someone disabled to model, or use their physical talents and abilities. The amazing Paralympians helped to change that in 2012 – and I hope I've played a part, too.

Being pregnant with my daughter Belle, who was born in 2014, presented me with new challenges. I felt I'd just regained control of my body, but when you're pregnant you have to surrender to it and so I had to let go again. All kinds of things happen physically and you can't do much about it. I missed exercising; I couldn't run and that was hard. But on the plus side, my caesarean was the easiest operation I've ever had, and I made a really speedy recovery. I was so used to dealing with operations that it posed no problem at all.

My body confidence journey has taken me from confident, to rock bottom, then back to confident again, but now it's a completely different type of confidence, which comes from a belief in my own body and its abilities. It's not so much about what's on the outside, though it's always great to feel good about how you look, but far more about what's on the inside – a deep-held respect for my body, a body I'm proud of and do my best to care for and keep healthy.

Choose Your Focus

What you focus on grows. If you think about a problem all the time, it starts to feel bigger than it really is. If you keep looking at your nose/hair/thighs in the mirror and worrying that they're too big, not the right shape or you have some issue with them, then you soon will have. But, on the other hand, if you focus on what you like about yourself, what you appreciate and value, that will be the feeling that grows, while the things you think of as problem areas will become less important.

Think hard about your good points. Have you got elegant hands, or thick shiny hair, or slim ankles, or lovely eyes, or an enviable cleavage? Focus on those good points and your thinking will become more positive. You can also maximise the things you do like about yourself. Wear a statement necklace to draw attention to your cleavage. Paint your nails a stunning colour to show off your hands. Treat yourself to a glorious new hairstyle.

If the things you don't like about yourself still trouble you, work out what issues you can change and which ones you just have to live with. For instance, if you hate being short or tall, there's not much you can do about that except to embrace your stature and make a conscious decision to enjoy it. But if you have a tummy that hasn't been the same since you had a baby, you might decide to join a gym, or go to an exercise class.

I believe in making the most of what you've got. What I don't believe in is feeling miserable about something you can't change. The way I see it, we come as a package. Good bits and not-so-good bits: it's all together in one body, and it's better to see ourselves as a whole rather than dissecting it into parts and then criticising certain features.

I have a friend whose hairline is receding and he hates it. He's not a shallow person, but it annoys him that he's going bald and he's not yet 40. I remind him that it's a natural process and we shouldn't be scared of the things that happen naturally as a part of living longer and getting older. Hair falls out when we get older, so why do we view that negatively when living a long and healthy life is something we all hope for? Some people don't get that luxury, so shouldn't we learn to see the effects of age as a privilege rather than a misfortune?

I often look at children's behaviour for inspiration. They accept people just as they are, they don't judge or think anything about us should be changed. Sometimes a child will ask me what happened to me and I say that I was poorly and had a lot of medicine to fix me and now I'm better, and thank you for asking. They always say, 'oh, OK,' and carry on chatting. That's how I'd like everyone to be: accepting towards ourselves and others.

Exercise – The Prototype

Try this exercise; it really helps combat self-critical feelings.

Look at yourself in the mirror and imagine that you are the first ever human being, the prototype for the species, and are therefore absolutely perfect.

Spend a couple of minutes looking at yourself calmly, peacefully and with wonder and delight. What a brilliant creation you are, what a wonderful piece of work. This is how a human being looks, and it's a miracle of invention, capable of sustaining, enduring and self-healing through the whole of a lifetime. Be delighted with yourself.

Eating Disorders

A healthy attitude to food is key to body confidence. What you put in is what you get out, so if you eat a good, balanced diet, then you're more likely to feel good, sleep well and look healthy.

Unfortunately, under pressure to conform to 'perfect' images, young people – women in particular – are vulnerable to eating disorders, most commonly anorexia, bulimia and binge-eating disorder. The number suffering has steadily increased in recent years, and many others are on the fringes of an eating disorder.

With anorexia nervosa, the most common eating disorder, the sufferer tries to keep their weight as low as possible, by starving themselves, exercising obsessively, or both. Because it involves starvation, anorexia also has the highest death rate of any mental illness.

Bulimia, also very common, is a condition in which the sufferer uses vomiting and laxatives to keep their weight down; and in binge-eating disorder (BED), more recently defined but also on the increase, the sufferer feels compelled to eat large amounts of food in a short space of time, regardless of whether they are actually hungry or not. Typically they feel disgusted with themselves after bingeing, and subsequently they try to cut down on food, which leads to a miserable and unhealthy cycle of alternately depriving and then stuffing themselves.

Any eating disorder really messes with the brain and can become a serious struggle. Once it's taken hold it is a psychological condition that needs proper treatment. If you suspect that you or anyone close to you has an eating disorder, do seek help. Start by going to your GP, who should refer you to a specialist clinic for eating disorders.

There's another condition that's sharply increasing at the moment, too, and that's Body Dysmorphic Disorder (BDD). It's not an eating disorder, but it has in common the distorted self-perception that is so often a hallmark of eating disorders.

People who have BDD become extremely anxious about their appearance. They tend to spend hours every day obsessing about some part of their body and come to see themselves as ugly, even when no one else perceives them in that way. It is a horrible illness to have, because it can dominate your life and cause real misery. But it is possible to find help and to recover.

For BDD and for all eating disorders there are support groups, books, websites and other sources of information and support, so you don't have to suffer alone. Help is just a click or a call away (see page 283).

Think Twice

As society increasingly conditions us not to accept ourselves, more and more people are going under the knife to 'fix' their bodies, spending money and taking big medical risks in the hope of improving the way they look.

Cosmetic surgery is on the increase. In 2015 the number of cosmetic procedures was 13 per cent higher than in the previous year. Nine out of ten people going under the knife are women, and most of them have breast augmentation, but the number of men opting for procedures has doubled and is still increasing. Liposuction – literally having fat sucked out – is common for both sexes, and so are rhinoplasty (nose jobs) and eye tucks.

I have to hold my hand up here. When I was 22 I had a boob job which took me from an A cup to a C cup. And I regret it. At the time I knew loads of people who'd had it done and I wanted to improve my chances of getting modelling and TV work and thought it would help. I loved the results at the time, but if I had to make the decision again I wouldn't do it. Now that I've had so many necessary cosmetic procedures, an unnecessary one seems like a needless risk, and to be honest, in my opinion breast implants just don't look real or natural – I should know, because I've got them!

While I would never tell anyone not to do something they have set their heart on, in most cases this type of surgery isn't life-changing in the way that people hope and dream it will be. Too many disappointed men and women subsequently try to reverse surgical changes, and when they can't they have to live with the regret of what they did to themselves.

I came across this a lot while filming the Channel 4 series *Bodyshockers*. I met people who wanted to make big changes to their bodies – not just surgical alterations but tattoos, implants, scarification (permanent scarring), and so on. I also talked to people who'd previously had procedures and now regretted them and were trying to get them reversed.

It's so easy to have procedures like this – the ads for them are everywhere, from the backs of magazines (alongside ads for nail salons and hair extensions) to posters on trains and buses, and with clinics now offering monthly payment plans, more and more young girls are seeing how easy and common it is and deciding that they can improve on what nature gave them. But most, like me, later come to regret it.

I'm grateful that I didn't have a huge, out-of-proportion augmentation – I've seen so many women who did and who, as a result, suffer from back problems, struggle to get clothes to fit and end up desperate for reversal surgery. That's possible in most cases, but it is expensive and, like any surgery, there are risks.

Now that I'm a mum, I see things very differently. I would feel sad if my daughter felt she needed breast augmentation at such a young age. The trouble is that as a society we no longer encourage acceptance. I've come across people who've had liposuction on their knees!

If you met someone you liked, whose personality attracted you, who was kind and fun and easy to talk to, would it put you off if their knees weren't perfect? I'm pretty sure it wouldn't. So before you have any kind of cosmetic procedure, think twice.

True Beauty

In interviews I'm sometimes asked whether I have a 'version' of beauty. For me, beauty is in the human spirit. If you are at a party and you see someone who is warm, funny, interesting and not in the least self-conscious, you gravitate towards them and want to talk to them. That kind of energy is so attractive, and it really doesn't matter too much what the person looks like.

On the other hand, you would never leave a meeting or a party and say, 'I was so touched and fascinated by that person's perfect nose, or smooth skin, or small waist.' We may briefly admire someone's features but then we forget them. And although we may not all have a perfect nose or waist, everybody has a human spirit and we can choose to let it shine.

A person who is comfortable and at ease with themselves is attractive. It's something we can sense and are drawn to. So rather than dislike things about yourself that are impossible to change, why not redirect your effort and energy into loving who you are and the body you have?

Someone who is not comfortable in their own body puts up barriers. For instance, if you don't feel good about your waist and someone puts their arm around it, you're going to tighten up and become tense, or move away. Without meaning to, you're going to come across as standoffish and cold, which is deeply unattractive.

I look at myself in the mirror and think, I am what I am. If I sat in front of the mirror and looked at individual parts of me and broke them all down and criticised them I would be there a very long time and then I'd walk away from the mirror feeling pretty bad.

So instead, I think of myself as a 'package' and I put energy into what I *can* change, and accept that in my package, just like anyone else's, there will be light *and* shade. And rather than homing in on the shade, I choose to let the light shine.

CHAPTER 4

Get Happy

Confident people are happier, and happy people feel more confident. So, to build confidence, it follows that you need to get happy!

I know, easier said than done. But I've come to realise that happiness isn't a luxury, it's a necessity, because without it everything else in life has very little meaning. Happiness is the ultimate currency; it's what we all want and pursue. Without it, money and fame are worthless; we only chase after those things because we believe they will make us happy. In fact, don't we do almost everything in our lives with the hope and intention of being happy? We buy a house, get married or choose a job because we think, or hope, it will make us happy.

So what *is* happiness? We can't try to acquire more of it if we don't completely understand what it is. Some people believe happiness is that feeling of being on a high, when something you've dreamed of works out, or when you win the lottery or your dream date says yes. Moments like this might feel magical, but that's all they are: moments. Truthfully, this kind of elation can't last more than a few hours before you bump back down to earth.

I believe that happiness is something much more enduring than a brief period of excitement. It's not just about achieving a goal, or feeling glad about a positive outcome; it's a long-term state of mind in which our life feels continuously purposeful, meaningful and worthwhile – not to mention enjoyable.

A lot of people believe they'll be happy at some point in the future, perhaps when they stop working so hard, or when they finally meet the right person, or have a child. But why shouldn't you be happy right now? Why shouldn't you experience a sense of fulfilment and satisfaction and even joy *today*, even if some of your dreams are yet to come true?

Too many of us live a life of unhappiness, believing that we aren't destined to be happy or that happiness lies just out of reach, or that we don't deserve the things that would make us happy. But why is that? We all deserve happiness, and we can all find it – not in dreams that may or may not be attainable, but in our day-to-day lives, right now.

In this chapter I'm going to look at what happiness is, why it so often seems out of reach and how we can all make happy a habit. I'll share some simple strategies that really help with this, and tips from experts who have discovered interesting – and sometimes surprising – things about what makes us happy and what does not.

We Can All Be Happy

Think everyone's either a happy person or not? That some people are wired for happiness and others missed out? Well, don't believe it. Happiness is a choice, and it's one that we can all make, no matter how unhappy we might have feel now or have felt in the past.

Scientific thinking about happiness has taken huge strides forward in recent years. Thanks to advances in medical scanning techniques, which demonstrate the brain impulses taking place in our head when we are feeling different emotions, neuroscientists now know that, far from being static or set in stone, the brain can continue to grow and form new connections throughout our lives.

As psychotherapist Christine Webber explains in her book *Get the Happiness Habit*:

> *Until a few decades ago, it was generally believed that once the brain was fully formed it could not be altered.*
>
> *Now we know that the brain has the potential to keep on changing throughout our lives – and that in response to us learning new things, it can alter the way it's 'wired'.*
>
> *The discovery that absorbing new information actually alters the circuitry of the brain has big implications for our ability to forge a happiness habit. And the great thing is that scientists are learning more all the time about the brain and how it can grow and develop – and how this can increase happiness.*
>
> *This research has encouraged many scientists to believe that we can 'activate' and therefore 'exercise' our brain just as we can train our bodies. Also, that by thinking joyful thoughts, we can build new connections, and strengthen the area of the brain which is linked to positive feelings of enjoyment.*
>
> *Does this then mean that by repeatedly focusing on happy*

things we can not only build up the areas of the brain that register happiness, but also, in time, make happiness easier to achieve? I think it does.

This is wonderful news. Our brains are so extraordinary that they can continue to absorb and change and adapt all through our lives. And what this means is that making the choice to learn happiness habits is a genuine option.

Happier

We don't have to make a black-and-white choice between being happy or sad. Life never works like that, does it? We can frequently feel happy *and* sad – as well as a whole range of other emotions – in the course of the same day.

The real decision is whether you want to move towards being generally happier, or move in the other direction, towards regular doom and gloom. It sounds like an obvious choice, but not everyone believes they can do it.

If you want to be happier, you really can be. You can shift your mind-set from discontented to cheerful. And you can do it in a surprisingly short space of time.

All kinds of things happen every day that can make us happy, if we stop to notice them. A nice cup of coffee, the sun coming out, a smile from a stranger, a hug from a friend, an appreciative word from your boss or a warm welcome from your pet when you walk through the door. These things bring real pleasure. So does a successful day at work, cooking a delicious meal, or perhaps digging the garden. Ordinary things can give us a sense of satisfaction.

KATIE PIPER

Being challenged to step up, and then achieving something –
whether that's your first five-kilometre race, successfully giving a
speech to a room full of people, or passing your driving test – can
feel wonderful. Pushing ourselves and achieving goals helps us see
our own potential, and this in turn makes us feel happy.

There's so much that we *can* be happy about, but sometimes
we don't even notice those things because we're too busy being
pessimistic, putting ourselves down or believing in bad luck. To
become happier, you need a shift in attitude, and a new way of
seeing things. You need to let happiness in.

Let Go of Unhappiness
Before you can start to be happy, you have to let go of unhappiness, because just as happiness can become a habit, so can
unhappiness.

Some suffering in life is unavoidable. It's not possible to be 'up'
all the time. Tears, loss, jealousy, pain and hurt: all of these are
part of life. Everyone has tough stuff to deal with; the small head-
aches of everyday life such as missing the bus, losing a favourite
item of clothing or dealing with a power cut. And then there are
the bigger difficulties, such as a close friend moving far away, a
relationship ending, or a serious health problem.

But the kind of unhappiness I'm talking about here is not short-
term sadness caused by specific events, it's more about attitude.
It's when you go through life saying things like, 'stuff always goes
wrong for me,' or 'I knew it wouldn't work out,' or 'I always get
picked on.'

Having a moan to a friend now and then is fine, but no one
wants to spend too much time around someone who seems

grudging or mean-spirited, who bats away every compliment or who continually whines and complains. It's exhausting and demoralising.

We all know people who love to play the 'yes, but' game, whose conversations often go like this:

Person A: 'I always feel ill the next day if I have too many alcoholic drinks.'

Person B: 'Why don't you set yourself a limit of two drinks then?'

A: 'Yes, but the trouble is I forget to keep count.'

B: 'Perhaps you could try soft drinks instead?'

A: 'Yes, but I just don't think I'd like them as much.'

B: 'Well, what about alternating a glass of water with each alcoholic drink? That helps a lot.'

A: 'Yes, but I'd just feel too bloated if I did that.'

B: 'OK, well what about trying low-alcohol drinks, they can be really nice?'

A: 'Yes, but it just wouldn't be the same, would it?'

You get the picture. B can go on making suggestions all day, but A has no intention of doing anything different; she just wants to complain.

This game was first identified by psychotherapist Eric Berne in his book *Games People Play,* and once you start trying to spot it you witness it happening all the time. It can be quite funny when you notice it, because the person playing A often has no idea that they're stalling person B (or sometimes several people) and they can go on and on.

Just make sure it isn't you playing the role of A! Choose *not* to be the person who says 'It's not fair', who stalls or finds excuses, or is mean-spirited. It's a sure-fire way to lose friends and make yourself miserable.

The Bigger Picture

To become happier, what we have to choose is our attitude to whatever comes along in life. Will we let things get us down, or will we take them in our stride? Will we think, 'typical, just my luck,' when something annoying happens, or will we think, 'never mind, it's not important.'

Some people take things very personally – they think everything is aimed at them, even if it's an innocent comment or gesture or an oversight that isn't intended to upset them at all. For instance, imagine you said hi to someone and they didn't respond. Would you decide that they didn't like you? Or would you tell yourself they were probably distracted and in fact didn't hear you?

We all have irrational thoughts at times, interpreting what goes on around us according to how we feel. If you're in a great mood you probably won't mind if someone seems to ignore you, whereas if you're having a rough day it may feel far more personal and hurtful.

As Christine Webber explains, in situations like this the approach known as CBT (Cognitive Behavioural Therapy) can provide us with some useful tools. CBT is all about finding ways to think more logically and rationally, by examining whether or not there is any evidence for the way we are automatically thinking.

Here's another extract from *Get the Happiness Habit,* which illustrates this point brilliantly:

The ABC Connection

The ABC connection is a very useful tool, often used by CBT therapists, and it certainly helps us to see the truth of what the Greek stoic philosopher Epictetus said: 'It's not things that upset us, it's our view of things.'

We all encounter events which adversely affect our moods. Just how much they affect our emotions depends on the 'automatic' thoughts that come into our minds in response to the scenario.

Here's an example.

Unexpectedly, a local infants' school was closed for the day because of burst pipes.

The situation of the school closing was identical for all the parents – in that the school was unavailable to them that day, and therefore they had to find alternative arrangements for their children.

But if we single out three mothers who all have five-year-old daughters at that school, we'll find that their reactions to the 'identical' event were all different.

Martha said: 'Oh God. That's all I need. I won't be able to go to work now. My boss hates me as it is. There's no one around to help me. Being a single mum is a complete nightmare … I'm going to have a panic attack …' Her overriding emotion, clearly, was one of high anxiety.

Elizabeth, on the other hand, said: 'Oh well, actually I'll enjoy having my daughter home for the day. I never seem to have enough time to do stuff with my kids individually. And since my son's school is open as normal today, I can seize this opportunity to go to the park with my daughter, and maybe do some baking too.' So, Elizabeth's emotional response to the unexpected school closure was a happy one.

61

Sonia was very upset. 'No!' she cried. 'This can't be happening. I'm supposed to be having a spa-day with my best friend. Why can't schools have better maintenance? Or why can't the teachers take the kids out for the day? It's all their fault. They're ruining everything!' I think that you could safely say that Sonia's emotion was one of anger.

So, as you can see, though the event was identical for these three mothers, their thoughts – and their subsequent emotional responses to the school closure – were very different.

This example teaches us that events in themselves don't cause emotions in us. Instead our emotional responses are caused by events, plus our own individual thoughts.

In cognitive behaviour therapy, we call this concept, 'The ABC connection'.

- **A** stands for the 'activating event'. In this case, it is that the school was unexpectedly closed for the day.
- **B** stands for beliefs and thoughts – which, as we have seen, were different in each woman, and were, almost certainly, thoughts that often cropped up in their minds.
- **C** stands for the 'consequent emotion' – which for Martha was high anxiety, for Elizabeth was happiness, and for Sonia was anger.

If we were to talk to each of these women we could find out what it was in their lives, or their beliefs, or backgrounds that was causing their particular thoughts.

Elizabeth did not upset herself at all about the school being closed. Instead, her automatic thoughts were positive. She appeared to see the sudden change in routine as an opportunity, rather than a *burden. Of course, it's possible that her life is easier than Martha's or Sonia's. But it's also likely she is someone with a healthy happiness habit who has appropriate self-regard and who also is able to be flexible.*

So, when we react badly to some happening, or to something that some person does or says, it can really help if we realise that this event in itself has not caused our distress, but that it was the event, coupled with what we believe or think, which caused our negative emotion.

When we can learn to analyse our thinking in this way, we can lessen our upset – and we can stop ourselves from plunging into unhappy emotions by looking at how our own thinking has contributed to them.

This makes perfect sense to me. I've tried the ABC test and it really does help. So next time you feel slighted, ignored, put down or hurt, try it and see whether it alters the way you feel about what happened.

Let Go of Perfection

Hands up if you're a bit of a perfectionist. There are a lot of us around, and I'm definitely one. I often find it hard to let go and relax, or to trust someone else to do the job. If I'm not careful, I can find myself still sorting, organising and preparing things late into the evening, extensive 'to do' list in hand. I often need reminding that being a perfectionist and being happy just don't go together.

The trouble is, perfectionism is a 'not-good-enough' state of mind. You give yourself (and everyone around you) a hard time because nothing is ever quite good enough. Your mind is filled with a lot of 'shoulds' and 'oughts' and 'must dos'. You're seldom at ease or contented and you rarely stop to smell the roses. Life for the perfectionist is about 'doing' rather than 'being' and it can become exhausting for you and for everyone around you.

Being a perfectionist normally leads to failure, because the truth is that life just isn't perfect. Things inevitably go wrong, certain things will get messed up and others just do not work out. But if you want to be happy, you need to be able to take these failures in your stride, laugh about them and move on.

Perfectionism can apply to relationships, too. There are people in good, healthy relationships who still believe there's someone better waiting just around the corner, simply because their mind-set is stuck on 'not good enough'.

Letting go of perfectionism isn't easy. It's often a deeply ingrained habit. But it is possible. If you commit to developing the habit of happiness, starting today, then bit by bit perfectionism will start to take a back seat to contentment. And who wouldn't want that?

Time and Happiness

In today's world it's all too easy to feel overwhelmed. Being short of time is a way of life for so many of us. We're always busy, always rushing, always trying to fit everything in – and predominantly failing to do so.

Having enough time is a vital component of happiness. Or, to put it the other way, if you constantly feel you don't have enough time, it's unlikely you'll be happy. Stressed, tired, irritable perhaps, but certainly not happy.

To be happy, you need to lose that feeling of having too much to do in too short a space of time. This, of course, is closely linked to perfectionism – it's us perfectionists who often feel we just don't have enough time to fit in all the things we think need to be done, as well as those who say 'yes' to everything and find themselves over-committed. With too many competing demands, we're unable to simply enjoy ourselves in the present moment. Our brains are ticking over with what has to be done next, and as a result we so often miss the magic and pleasure that lies in something right before our eyes – a child's hug, a beautiful sunset, a favourite piece of music.

Time-pressure, when it's your way of life, can easily lead to depression, as you find yourself buried under a mountain of burdens. The only way out is to simplify life and slow down. There isn't a shortcut to this; you have to choose which of those burdens to cast off, whether that's by delegating a job to someone else, saying no to something or finding a way to simplify it.

It's about prioritising – choosing some of your life's activities and letting others go. I know, you're thinking, 'But I can't let anything go, it's all vital.' Well, believe me, it isn't. Make a list of everything you do in a day and a week, then look at what you could change. Keep the things that do you good – don't ditch your exercise class, for instance – but get rid of some of the things that don't bring you any benefit; cut back on the cleaning, delegate the washing up, let your family sort out their own laundry or sports kit and do your shopping online.

Developing Happiness Habits

So, now to the crunch – what do we actually need to do to become happier? The answer is simple, really: we need more of what does us good in life.

There are three steps:

One: *Identify what makes you happy.*

Two: *Get your life into balance, with plenty of the things that make you happy.*

Three: *Develop new habits.*

One: Identify What Makes You Happy

This might take a little time. You need to stop being so busy and have a think about it.

For instance, you might enjoy spending time with your family, going to a particular exercise class or for a run, having meals out with friends, a leisurely chat with a good friend on the phone, bonding with your pet, indulging in a good read, cooking a delicious meal from scratch. These are all things that psychologists say improve our SWB – Sense of Wellbeing.

For me, happiness is when I'm living in the moment, completely absorbed in what's happening: those times, in fact, when I never stop to think 'I'm happy' because I'm too busy living life. What is it that absorbs you so deeply that you don't notice time pass?

There are a few things that almost always, for almost all of us, boost happiness. So if you're stuck for ideas about what makes you happy, try these:

Exercise – There's a proven link between exercise and a sense of wellbeing, but you have to get *enough* exercise, and that means an absolute minimum of half an hour a day. Choose anything you fancy: walk, run, skip, cycle, go to the gym or take a class. It all works.

Laugh – Humour, and laughter, are just so important. My dad is always laughing and joking and in my darkest times that really helped me. My husband Richie is similar. He makes me laugh and I love that. When I felt down because I had to wear plastic tubes up my nose for two years, Richie decided to keep a diary of all the places my tubes had been. He'd give me a present and say, 'Careful you don't get so excited that your tubes shoot out!' His humour normalised it, and made a difficult experience into a loving joke between us.

Do something for someone else – taking your mind off yourself and doing someone else a favour can be an instant Sense of Wellbeing boost. You could buy someone a coffee, give a busker a coin and a smile, tell a friend how great they look, or offer to carry someone's shopping for them.

Two: Get Your Life into Balance
This also takes some thought, because no matter how happy something makes you, you don't want or need it all the time. For instance, say you love your spin class. That doesn't mean you want to do it every day – twice a week might be enough for you. Or perhaps you love curling up in front of the TV with a slice of chocolate cake. But you wouldn't do it all day every day, it's a joy because it's a treat.

Balance is about making sure you do what you need to do – go to work, pay the bills, and so on – and alongside that you also do plenty of the things that make you happy. Of course, going to work might be one of your happy things, and if it is, you're blessed, since work takes up a good chunk of the week. But even doing a job you enjoy can make you unhappy if you're spending too many hours there. Take a good look at the balance of your life; it might even be worth writing down how long you spend on the different activities in your week.

Getting the balance right will almost certainly involve some trial and error. You need to pay close attention to how the activities in your life make you feel, and try shifting things towards the happier side of the scales. It might take only a small adjustment to make you a lot happier. Something like leaving work half an hour earlier a couple of times a week so that you can spend more time with your child, or get to the gym.

Three: Develop New Habits

You don't have to think much about something that's a habit, you just do it. Like cleaning your teeth, or feeding the dog, or setting your alarm. These things, and dozens of other things that you do during your week, are automatic, because you've programmed yourself to do them.

Happiness habits need to be the same. If what's missing in your life is exercise and you want to go running three times a week, you have to consciously prioritise it until it becomes a habit. Experts say this can take between two weeks and three months. Stick with it, especially when you don't feel like doing it; the habit will form and your happiness levels will naturally be boosted.

The Courage to be Happy

One story I just love is about a woman called Brenda Finn. Brenda is a children's entertainer, she makes people – small people, and quite a few bigger ones, too – happy for a living. And to me she represents true courage. Brenda had more reason than most people to feel pretty sorry for herself, but she made the decision to choose happiness and, with her gorgeous smile and sparkling eyes, she's one of the happiest people I know. She's bright, interesting and a lot of fun to be around. But it could all have been so different.

When she was fourteen, Brenda woke up one day to find half her hair lying on her pillow. Within days all of her hair had fallen out. Brenda was devastated, and when doctors told her she was suffering from alopecia and that her hair might never grow back, she felt as though her life was over.

'For the next two years I refused to leave the house. I was home-schooled and I lost all my friends. I had been a cheeky, outgoing kid but I changed completely. I felt I'd lost my teenage years, I couldn't be like other girls and I just sat for hours in front of the TV. My mum tried to get me to go out, but I refused. I was in denial about what had happened. I wore a wig, even at home, and I refused to look at myself.'

When she was sixteen and had taken her GCSEs, Brenda realised she was going to have to go out, or else spend the rest of her life indoors. It was a pretty grim prospect for anyone, let alone someone so young. So she started working as a volunteer in a local nursery.

'I felt safe there,' she says, 'little children are so accepting. After a few months I was so comfortable with them that I could take the wig off and let them play with it. The other nursery workers were fine with it, too, and I began to realise that not everyone is judgemental, people aren't born that way, they make a choice to be.'

Brenda went on to work as an elf in a Christmas show – 'lots of costume changes, we all wore wigs and no one was looking at me, so that was fine. And when the show ended the manager suggested I audition to be a redcoat at Butlins.

'I was terrified, but I made myself go, and after four rounds of auditions in which I had to do magic tricks and tell jokes, I got the job. I was amazed. It meant working in Skegness, a long way from my home in London, so I almost didn't go, but my mum said that if I went I could come home at any time and it wouldn't be a failure. She said part of success is just trying.'

What a lovely mum. With her encouragement, Brenda went to Skegness and she loved her new job. 'I rediscovered a part of me that I thought I'd lost,' she says. 'It brought back the fun, chatty, outgoing side of me. I began to relax and tell people the truth and most people just accepted me.'

Today Brenda lives with her musician fiancé Wayne and she's in great demand for children's parties, as well as to perform in hospitals and at shopping centres.

'I'm happy because I have a job I love and a great guy and I don't worry about being bald. Sometimes I wear a wig and sometimes I don't. On a hot day I'll go to the shops without it. When Wayne and I first started dating, I had to tell him. He hadn't worked it out, even though my hair would change dramatically from one day to the next. When I explained he was fascinated and now he loves the way I can change how I look.

'Most people are fine with it, and if I come across the occasional idiotic comment I just walk away. I've realised that you can choose how you deal with things. Now I lead a packed life – I'm still making up for all the time I spent at home in front of the TV.'

Brenda is right: we all have a choice in life. She chose happiness. What will you choose?

The Power of Happiness

I also love this little story from Christine Webber's book:

> A child aged about two was travelling on the London Underground with her mother. She was a lively and engaging little girl and so infectiously happy that everyone who came into the carriage caught her eye and started smiling and laughing.
>
> I watched carefully as her impact spread amongst the commuters. A city gent began to play peekaboo with her from behind his Financial Times. Two schoolboys, who had been arguing amongst themselves, started chatting to her instead. A dour-faced woman glanced up from her paperback and pulled faces at the little girl, who chuckled delightedly in response. And a tired-looking workman, obviously on his way home from a night shift, sang a funny song with her before he got off the train.
>
> This was one of the most compelling illustrations of the power of happiness that I have ever seen. And I know that most of those commuters left the tube that morning feeling jollier and brighter than when they had entered the train – and all because of their contact with this child. Sheer energetic joy poured out of her and I'm convinced that even though she was so young, she somehow had a sense of the influence she was having on

those around her. I can only hope that she never loses her
happiness habit.

Children just innately know how to be happy. As the mum of a toddler, I constantly see how full of wonder and delight a small child is, and how they light up your day. We can learn so much from them.

Happiness, as this story shows, is infectious. And it isn't just children who can spread it. A recent study found that if your friend is happy about something, you are likely to be happier, too. We love being around happy people, and we love having a reason to feel happy.

All you need, in the end, is the willingness to be happy; to let the good things be the biggest part of your day. And the happier you feel, the more confident you will be, because the two sensations are inextricably linked.

CHAPTER 5

My Normal

We all want to be 'normal', don't we? But what *is* normal?

I sometimes wonder how many people actually feel they are completely normal. So many of us, for one reason or another, believe that we don't quite fit in, belong or conform to whatever we imagine normal to be. Scratch the surface and a lot of us have a sense that something about us doesn't quite meet the standards and expectations of society.

According to its definition, being normal means conforming to something that is standard, typical, average, expected or usual. In other words, it's the opposite of unusual or different. But who decides what is 'standard'? And doesn't it change from one day to the next? Fashions change, our attitude to body shape changes, our ideas of what is and isn't beautiful change. So the picture of normal is a constantly moving one.

Every one of us is different from the next person, and in general we like being different; most of us wouldn't want to be identical to someone else, and nor do we want to be considered typical, average or ordinary. We all like to think we're just a little bit special. That's why I've come to the conclusion that normal is whatever you happen to be. And if you're a bit different from the next person, that's fine, because that's your normal.

'You're not normal' is used as an insult because it assumes that we all want to be the same. But actually what I think we want is not to be singled out, criticised or picked on for our differences, whatever they may be.

The trouble is that instead of accepting that we're all normal, and that we all deserve appreciation and acceptance for who we are, we've fallen into the trap of comparing ourselves with what we think we 'should' be. And that's a recipe for discontent, self-criticism and misery, because we can't change who we are and how we look.

I know what it's like to feel normal, one of the crowd, to conform to accepted standards of prettiness. And I also know what it's like to feel different and to be stared at and criticised because of it.

Many of us have scars. Mine are highly visible, and so are a lot of other people's. But for some, the scars are internal. Those people can feel just as different as someone who has a visible difference on the outside. They too are struggling for a sense of normal.

I used to take normal for granted, and then, after the attack, I spent years fighting my way back towards a sense of normal, both physically and mentally. Now I take nothing for granted, but I do, at last, once again feel normal. And that's because I've learned that whatever I am, however my life is, that's my normal.

I know, from the many people I meet and speak to through my work, that the feeling of being different, unhappy and uncomfortable is very common. So many of us feel that something about us is wrong or needs changing and that in some way we are not normal.

The reasons why any of us might feel we don't fit in are so many. Of course there are outer differences, those visible differences that are instantly noticeable: disfigurements and disabilities. Then there are racial and size differences. And then there are the inner differences: depression, mental illness, phobias, fear and loneliness.

When we don't feel normal, our confidence levels can hit rock bottom. So this chapter is about exploring what normal is, and how we can each, in our own unique and special way, feel that we are just as normal as the next person.

Losing Normal

I once knew what it was like to feel normal. For 23 years I fitted in; I could walk, talk, smile and function like the majority of other people. I took my health and my perfectly average, reasonably nice, looks for granted. And although I didn't know it at the time, I liked feeling normal. Of course I wanted to stand out, too – I wanted to be a TV presenter and model, so I worked hard to make the best of myself and get others to notice me. But I had no understanding of what it would be like to truly stand out, or to feel singled out by society.

Then came the attack, which left me fighting for my life. As I began my recovery I was already acutely aware of how much 'normal' I had lost.

Imagine not being able to smile. A smile is the basis of communication with other people; it's something we take for granted every day. But because the skin grafts on my face were extremely tight and inflexible, at first I couldn't make any facial expressions and I certainly couldn't smile. For around two years I could feel happy, angry or sad inside but I couldn't express it on my face. It was a very odd experience, and because I knew people couldn't work out what I was feeling by looking at me, I tended to keep my head down and avoid eye contact. I felt I was losing my personality and my sense of who I was. I couldn't show others that I was excited, frustrated, puzzled, doubtful, amused or being flirtatious. My face was a blank.

The first time I was able to smile again was when I went to a burn rehabilitation and scar management clinic in France for intensive therapy to help improve my burns and scars. For two years I had felt that the skin on my face was so tight, but suddenly it started to feel looser and at last I could smile again, which in turn gave me even more reason to smile! My new smile was a bit lopsided and it wasn't my old smile, but to me it was amazing. I got one of the nurses to take a photo of me smiling and I printed it on an A4 piece of paper and took it with me when I flew home a couple of days later. I showed my mum the picture at the airport and told her, 'I got my smile back!'

That was a big step back towards normal for me, and there were many others along the way. I was determined to fight my way back to normality. I loved life, I loved the life I had had, and then someone suddenly tried to take it away from me. They wanted to destroy me, but from the moment I began my recovery I was determined that they wouldn't succeed. I had lost normal, I had almost lost my life, but I was going to rebuild it and replace what I had with a new life and a new normal.

Don't Let What Happens Define You

Many people feel that they are different to others because of something they have experienced – an accident, illness, loss or trauma of some kind. It could be a divorce, a family rift, a financial crisis or a physical trauma.

If you've undergone some kind of change in your life that has deeply affected you, then it's hard not to feel as though what happened then, defines you now. Whether or not you look the same as before, you may now feel that you are different, that what has happened has marked you out and that you are no longer normal and don't blend into the crowd or fit in as you once did. As a result you might find yourself making assumptions about the rest of your life, and other people may do so, too.

After what happened to me, many people saw my future as narrow and restricted. I didn't blame anyone for thinking this way – it was understandable – but I refused to go along with this view. I wanted my life back, and I didn't want what had happened to define me; I wanted to make up my own definition of me.

I was determined that the attack should become just a tiny blip in my life, insignificant in comparison to what came afterwards. I was still alive, and I would go on and I would fight for my right to a good life. Of course it wasn't going to be the same as the life I had had before – nothing would ever be the same, and I knew I couldn't try to make it the same. I had to let go and move on, and in some ways that was exciting because I didn't know what lay ahead.

I hadn't been able to wear any of my old clothes for two years because I had had tubes coming out of my stomach, and by the time I could wear them, I no longer wanted to, because they reminded me of my former life and the girl I used to be. So I sold a lot of them on eBay. I liked writing all the descriptions and taking the photos, I felt like a fashion journalist. I had nothing much to do at the time, I couldn't work or even leave the house, other than for medical appointments, so I spent a lot of time following the auctions and bids, and packing things up to be sent off, which gave me satisfaction. It was closure. Just throwing things out would have felt defeatist, as if the attackers had taken away my past, but selling things felt good. I had no money at the time; I was on disability benefit so the money was a big deal. I would sell something for £30 and think, wow!

My mum had to pay for the hospital parking for my appointments, for the congestion zone charges (the hospital was in London) and for my prescriptions, so if I made some money I would pay for those things myself that month, and it lifted my spirits. So selling my clothes had a double benefit: it made me a bit of money and gave me a good way to let go of my old life.

Collecting cosmetics did me a lot of good, too. I'd been a trained beautician and had had bags of beauty products in the London house I'd shared with friends. After the attack, my housemates were advised by the police to move straight out, so they hastily put some of my stuff in bags, but they didn't have time to grab everything and inevitably a lot of the cosmetics were lost.

For ages afterwards, I had nothing. Those products would have been wasted on me anyway; what had once been my beauty drawer was now full of Vaseline, bandages, steroid creams and pressure garments.

But then, slowly, I started to collect nice things again. I was given a lovely eye cream as a present and I treasured it. As I slowly built up a new collection of cosmetics and creams I looked after them with real care, cleaning the bottles and storing them nicely, because to me they represented my journey back to normality.

I used to get lots of nice things for my feet and legs, because they were undamaged. A 'beauty night' would involve shaving, exfoliating, moisturising and fake-tanning my legs and painting my toe nails, because it was too painful to do anything to my upper body. It was the same when I started to exercise again: I had a great toned bum, thighs and calves because for three years all I could do was lower-body exercises like lunges and squats.

Once I started to go out again and try to build myself a new social life, so much had changed there, too. Most of my old friends had moved on in their lives; many were getting married and having children, while at the age of 27 I felt like a girl who was only just leaving home for the first time. I'd done it once, at 18, and now I had to do it all over again. And this time I had to do it complete with burns and scars.

Navigating the world of work, friends and independent living was hard. At times it was terrifying and I wanted to run back to my parents' home and hide. But what kept me going, even when people made cruel comments or stared at me, was the determination that I would not let the men who hurt me win; I would not let what happened define me, and I would not give in to despair. I was going to have a life: a full, rich and interesting life. And I was going to collect new memories, good ones that would outnumber the painful ones.

Sometimes when awful things happen we open other doors and

go down other paths. Not the paths we were once on, but new ones that lead to new places – places that can be just as good or even better than the ones we were headed to before.

If your life has changed, if you feel that an event in your life has taken over, you *can* make the decision not to let it define you.

Sometimes it is the invisible scars that are hardest to heal. When you have visible scars you tackle them head-on because you have to if you want to move forward. But you can hide the invisible ones; people don't know you are hurting, so these wounds are often never addressed. And that's dangerous, because without some kind of healing process it's hard to reclaim your life and move forward. But whatever it was that happened to you, the essence of you, your spirit, is the same and you can move beyond the painful memories to a new and worthwhile life.

Why Me?

Through my charity I meet a lot of people whose lives have been changed by an accident – a car crash, a fire, an explosion. People who've been burned and scarred and who ask, 'Why did it happen to me?'

In fact, I don't think there's one of us who hasn't asked that at some point about something. Life can seem horribly unfair at times. Why did you fail to get the job/man/woman of your dreams? Why did you have the accident/lose the money/miss out on that great flat?

But when it comes to 'Why me?' there's another – much more positive – way of looking at it. Perhaps the answer to the question is: 'Because I'm strong enough to take it.

I used to think, 'Why did this happen to me?' and in the end I decided, 'Well, why not me? Perhaps I can be glad it was me, and not someone else. I wouldn't want it to be my sister or my friend or even a stranger on the street.'

I have strong spiritual beliefs, which have helped me a lot through the darkest times. And in looking at what happened to me I realised that I could cope with it. Perhaps it happened because I had the strength to get through it and maybe another person might not have survived it. That gives me comfort. It's a rationale that works for me, and perhaps it can work for you.

Having survived, I feel passionately about doing some good in the world, by changing the taboo around disfigurement. It seems to me that it's one of the last remaining taboos and I want to show the world that people with scars should be treated normally, just as someone of a different race or a different size would be.

I'm always going to look the way I do now. The doctors have done an amazing job – and continue to, because I'll be having operations for the rest of my life – but basically this is me, and how I am now is my new normal.

I've been known to go directly from a speaking engagement to hospital, to have surgery such as a graft from my buttocks to create a new inner lining for my nose, and then get up the next day, do my hair and make-up in the hospital and still keep an appointment or even deliver a speech. I'll be smiling and, yes, I'm sore, but this is my life and it's a life I have come to appreciate. I have got to the position now that I look in the mirror and think, I am what I am and it's not that bad.

When I made the shift from 'Why me?' to 'Why not me?' it helped me a lot. I stopped searching for answers I was never going to find and began to think forward to 'This is me now, so what am I going to do about it?' I felt instantly less helpless, more in charge of my life, and much more confident. Because although I couldn't change what had happened, I could do something about what would happen next. I could stand up as a woman who had been attacked and say, 'You didn't defeat me.' And having accepted the situation, I could put my energy into recovering and doing something to help other people suffering in similar ways.

Social Attitudes

What I want for myself, and for the many other people who have suffered disfigurement through burns and other injuries, is for us to be accepted without prejudice, scorn or criticism.

If you are trying to teach your child not to be alarmed by people with scars and burns, as I am and as so many other parents are, then Halloween and images of scarred people as baddies in Disney cartoons are going to make it difficult for you. If we're conditioned to see anyone with scars as evil, then life is going to be a lot tougher for those of us who do have this kind of outer physical difference.

I have to admit that I don't like Halloween these days. I'm fine with people dressing up as a cat or a wizard, but the trend towards fake scars, blood and gore seems to me like a backward step.

I'd like us to teach our kids that it's normal to be scarred, disfigured or disabled. It's a taboo that I hope will be defeated within my lifetime. I would like my daughter and her friends to think it's absolutely unacceptable to insult, criticise or pick on someone because they look in any way different.

I don't doubt that the 'scars are evil' attitude contributes to online trolling. Almost anyone with an online presence nowadays is at the receiving end of a bit of trolling – the posting of unkind, critical and cruel comments, often anonymously – but social prejudices only help to reinforce it. Generally if this happens to me I ignore it, but recently I had a comment so nasty that I was prompted to reply, 'You seem so angry and unhappy. Imagine if you turned that anger around, you could have such a happy existence.' The woman didn't reply. Her comment was a reflection of her opinion of herself, as trolls' comments usually are, and it's a shame, because instead of lashing out against others, she could be spending her time and energy making her own life happier.

I'd like to see a lot more tolerance, kindness and understanding in the world, and, of course, online. The more we accept our own differences and difficulties, the more we'll accept other people's and the better the world will be.

And I'd like to see society – that's all of us – celebrate all differences and be inclusive of all people, so that no one feels they are alone, isolated or at risk of criticism.

Fake It to Make It

Back in the real world, where people still gasp, stare, whisper to each other or make thoughtless comments, I learned early on in my recovery to do all I could to put others at ease. I wanted to be sociable, to meet people and to have a social life that included going to bars, restaurants and concerts, so I would try to make people feel comfortable around me, by showing them that I am comfortable with myself.

I think of this as 'fake it to make it' confidence. It's a tool in my confidence toolbox that can be really useful. I may feel nervous and apprehensive going out to meet new people, but I try to make a joke and get them laughing, to break the ice and show them that I'm fine with how I look and they should be too.

If I was going to meet friends who had people with them that I hadn't met before, I know my friends wouldn't say, 'Katie is coming, she is burned, don't mention it, don't look at her arm, just to warn you.' They know I will turn up smiling, have a laugh and maybe even make a joke about myself to put everyone at ease.

There was a stage when everybody I met just talked about the weather. They didn't want to say anything about me, and they wouldn't tell me their day-to-day thoughts and problems because they felt that anything happening in their lives was trivial compared to what had happened to me. It was awful! They would start every sentence with, 'It's nothing compared to what you are going through,' when all I wanted was for them to relax and tell me about their abandoned diet or their annoying boyfriend or how they hated their haircut. I wanted everything to be normal, trivial, easy, because that way I could forget about me and enjoy being with other people. So sometimes I made a fool of myself to make people feel comfortable, or pretended to be loud and confident when I certainly didn't feel that way. But it worked. I walked the walk and talked the talk and my confidence grew. Sometimes you have to make things happen and pretend to be what you want to be until – before you know it – it becomes real. Behave in a certain way and you'll start to feel that way.

Run Your Own Race

I believe that each of us can only aspire to be the best version of ourselves, and then get on with our lives without comparing ourselves to anyone else. Constant comparisons and competitiveness only lead to discontent, so I made a decision pretty early on in my recovery not to compare myself to anyone else, or to consider myself as different. The way I look is the way I am, it's my normal. And this is true for each of us, we are all normal. Claim your normal, and live with your scars, inner or outer, without comparing yourself to anyone else. And don't forget that the person you see who seems to have it all may be hiding scars of their own.

The only competition you need to have in life is to strive to achieve your personal best. The only race you are running is your own, and if you can be satisfied with that, you will be happy. I set myself high standards – in my exercise, my work and in coping with operations and medical procedures. I don't waste time feeling sorry for myself; I make the most of what I have.

Someone once said to me, 'Worry is a total waste of time, all it does is steal your joy.' Many people get stuck in an unhappy cycle of envy, dissatisfaction and misery through comparing themselves to someone or something they can never be. So enjoy what you do have, and stop navel-gazing! Of course you are allowed to feel sorry for yourself, but set a limit and then take your mind off yourself by getting involved in something else.

To forget about yourself for a bit and stop thinking about how you look can be so liberating.

Life is exciting. We have a limited amount of time on this planet, and there are so many things we can plan and do, and wonderful people we can meet. We can – and should – choose to be around people who make us feel good.

One of the things that attracted me to Richie was that he seemed to enjoy life so much. I thought, 'That's who I want to be around.' I loved his energy and I've become a happier person for being around him – it's infectious.

Tulsi's Normal

Tulsi Vagjiani is a brilliant example of someone who doesn't waste time feeling sorry for herself and who has found her own, happy normal. I first met her when she came along to the Foundation and from the start I found her courage and confidence impressive.

Tulsi had good reason to feel that the world was a harsh place. At the age of ten she was travelling to India with her parents and brother when their plane crashed. Her parents and brother died and Tulsi, helped to safety by another passenger, suffered serious burns to her face and body.

Tulsi went to live with her grandparents and over the next five years she had numerous skin grafts.

As a teenager coping with looking different, Tulsi struggled. 'I had no confidence, I was full of self-doubt. I kept looking at others and thinking, "I wish I could look like that or I wish I could do that"', she told me. 'Someone would make an unkind remark like, "You look ugly" and it would send me into a spiral of misery. I struggled to feel good about myself or to have any self worth.'

As a teenager, Tulsi attended a burns camp in the States, because there was nothing like it in the UK. It was a fantastic experience.

'It was great and it taught me a lot,' she says. 'Seeing other people find the courage to push themselves to do things like abseiling and climbing made me decide to push myself, too.'

Back home, Tulsi studied for a psychology degree, before going on to take a second degree in applied health science, which she achieved despite constant health problems. At 26 she developed kidney failure and had to begin nightly dialysis, which went on for three years, until she was given a transplant.

As a result of an immune system weakened by so much medication, Tulsi suffered infections and brittle bones. But she got through it all, finished her studies and then took a long, hard look at her life.

'I needed to move on with my life and put the crash behind me,' she explains. 'It was time to see the accident and the burns as something that had happened to me and not to let it control my life.'

Tulsi began working as a Pilates teacher. 'I'd been doing Pilates for a while and I loved it,' she says. 'It gave me body confidence and allowed me to exercise in a way that didn't cause me any pain.'

As her health improved and her practice became established, Tulsi decided to get in touch with us at the Foundation, where we were able to offer her treatments including hair restoration and eyebrow tattooing. Tulsi was delighted.

'I had always wanted eyebrows. And when I finally got some they defined my face. And the hair weave was fantastic. The treatments helped my confidence enormously.'

Tulsi, 37, now works with us at the Foundation, representing us at charity events and sharing her story. She's a great speaker and a great advertisement for the confidence that comes from having found her own normal.

'I've finally accepted my scars and I don't want to hide them,' she says. 'I feel good about myself and I don't let unkind comments get me down. I am as normal as the next woman, I love clothes and make-up. I used to think my appearance was everything, but I know now that I'm more than just what's on the outside.'

Choose Who You Want To Be

'I am who I choose to be.'

That's the mantra I live by. And, rather than letting other people tell us what to think and be, or following the crowd like sheep, I believe that we should choose for ourselves how we want to be and what we believe.

Who can tell us what should be attractive and desirable? Who made up the rule that beauty has to be symmetrical, proportional, flawless?

Beliefs don't exist unless we give them life. So in my home I'm not disabled, I'm just a wife and mum; my partner finds me attractive, my daughter sees me as Mummy and we are a normal family having happy times.

I think you have to choose – are you going to have your life dictated by strangers or are you going to live it your way? I've asked myself that many times. And there's no doubt in my mind about the answer. My life is what I make it.

I choose to focus on the good in life, the people who thank me for setting an example or for putting things in perspective for them, the people who show kindness and goodness to others.

You have to get to the point when you ask yourself who is in charge of your life. Is it strangers, the media and the people who judged or rejected you, or is it in fact you?

We are mentally unbreakable if we choose to be. Those who have endured real hardship – those suffering in wars and so many other experiences – are testimony to this. We are fragile beings but ultimately we are unbreakable.

You can make yourself whatever you want to be. And I hope that you'll start by deciding that however you are right at this moment is normal. *Your* normal.

CHAPTER 6

Beyond Comfort

We each of us have the ability to do amazing things. We are capable of surprising ourselves, and others, with what we can create and achieve. We have the potential to show strength and resilience, to endure and overcome suffering and to accomplish the stuff of our dreams. Yet all too often we hold ourselves back, convincing ourselves that we're small, unimportant or insignificant. And when we think this way, we stop ourselves from going beyond what feels comfortable and trying new things.

No one likes it when things get uncomfortable, but sometimes it's good for us to push ourselves past our 'working edge' – that point where our comfort zone ends and the unknown begins. Yes, it can make us sweat with apprehension, lose sleep and feel afraid, but pushing yourself to achieve something new, something beyond your usual expectations, can feel wonderful; it's the biggest confidence boost I know. And that confidence increases: once you have tried something new, you feel more able to go on to the next thing, and the next.

In this chapter I'm going to challenge you to step beyond your comfort zone and begin to find out exactly what you are capable of achieving. It's something I know a fair bit about. During my recovery there have been many points when I wanted to stay exactly where I was and not try anything new or different. When I finally got back to my parents' house after months spent in hospital, I never wanted to have to leave again. For a while I thought I would just live inside the safe limits of those walls, where I was with the people who loved me and where I wouldn't have to face strangers or the outside world, with all its dangers, judgements and obstacles. The first time my dad suggested I go out with him and Mum to the pub for a drink, I wanted to refuse. Why would I do something so scary, when I could just stay indoors? But Dad knew that I needed to challenge myself, and very gently he encouraged me to go.

Eventually I agreed, and although my heart was pounding and I felt very unsafe and uncomfortable, I made it to the pub and sat quietly at a corner table with my parents. And nothing terrible happened. In fact, much to my relief, the other people in the pub didn't seem to notice me. Afterwards, we walked home and I felt a real sense of achievement. I had taken a step forward and, small as it was, it represented the possibility of a future I had thought was lost.

Flash forward a couple of years, to the first time I agreed to give a talk in front of an audience. I had launched the Katie Piper Foundation and in order to raise funds I needed to go out and tell people about what had happened to me and what I hoped to do for others in a similar position. As I waited to walk into the room and listened to the audience chatting away, I thought, 'What have I done?' It was terrifying. But afterwards, as the audience applauded and I realised I had managed it, I felt fantastic – it was a feeling so good I wished I could bottle it.

That feeling, when you know that you've achieved something you had once believed wasn't possible, is what builds confidence. And it's what I believe we all deserve and can have, as long as we find the courage to step beyond comfort.

What is Our Comfort Zone?

Our comfort zone, essentially, is the activities and behaviours in our everyday lives that cause us minimum stress and risk. When we operate within our comfort zone we feel secure and safe. We may experience a little anxiety here and there, but not much, and when operating from within our comfort zone we perform steadily, with no great lows or highs.

You're in your comfort zone when you do the everyday things you don't have to think about much. Things like cooking dinner, travelling to work and watching TV.

There is nothing wrong with having a comfort zone, it's part of life and it's natural for us to spend most of our time there. We all need time without being overly anxious or stressed – living in a permanent high state of stress or taking constant risks would be awful.

Our comfort zone is often a nice place to be; it's easy and pleasant. But not always. Sometimes a comfort zone is anything but comfortable and far from good for us. For instance, living with an abusive or violent partner can become the norm, the state you are used to, but that doesn't make it all right. And of course overeating can be part of your comfort zone, a habit that becomes a way of life. I talked to a nutritional therapist recently about food and comfort zones and she told me that people who eat, say, half a dozen biscuits because they're miserable after a bad day at work tend to feel comforted for only the briefest time. In fact, the comfort lasts just about as long as they have the taste of the biscuits on their tongue. Once they've swallowed the last one, far from feeling satisfied, they frequently feel a real sense of failure. So feeling a failure becomes that person's 'comfort' zone.

Drinking too much, using drugs, being in an unhappy relationship or job: all of these can be what we are used to, and despite the fact that they make us unhappy, they're habitual and familiar, and therefore low-stress in comparison to the unknown.

Why Step Outside Your Comfort Zone?

We all have a comfort zone, both practically and emotionally, and while we need it and it's part of life, we also need to summon up the courage to step outside it from time to time.

If your comfort zone includes aspects of life that are far from comfortable and far from good for you, then changing them makes sense. For the man or woman in an abusive relationship, ending it may be hard, but it's vital if you're to have the life you deserve. For the person who overeats, changing the habit may be a big challenge, but it will reap huge benefits – both physically and emotionally.

It's perhaps harder to see why you should step outside your comfort zone if it's actually not doing you any harm and is, mostly anyway, a pretty nice place to be. If you like your job, your relationship and your lifestyle, why would you change anything?

Here are five reasons why stepping outside your comfort zone can be the best thing you ever did:

One: You Will Learn New Things

Doing something new increases the memory and makes our brains more malleable, or more versatile and open to learning. In other words, stepping outside your comfort zone will be good for your brain, helping to keep it sharp, receptive and retentive.

When we try new things, we grow as people – especially when those new things involve a bit of anxiety and unease. Take learning to surf. It might seem totally daunting at first, dangerous and difficult, but stick with it and the first time you manage to stand on your board and take a wave, you will feel exhilarated and so proud of yourself, with a huge sense of accomplishment. That's a feeling you will never achieve by staying inside your comfort zone.

Two: You Will be More Productive

When we're in the comfort zone we tend to do the minimum that's necessary. We lose drive and ambition, we don't push ourselves. We can be busy, or seem to be busy, but sometimes busy is a way of avoiding doing anything new. When we step outside our comfort zone we learn to work better, achieve more and find new ways to get things done.

Three: You Will Find it Easier to Cope with Change

From inside your comfort zone, change can seem scary and definitely something to avoid. But if we try always to steer clear of any fear and uncertainty in life, we're doomed to fail. It's not possible to stay forever in a carefully controlled safety zone; fear and uncertainty are inevitable at some point. And if we choose to step outside our comfort zone, and to make changes, we are practising for them. Which means that when change that we haven't chosen happens, we'll be better able to cope with it. To put it simply: planned change helps prepare you to cope with change that you didn't plan.

Four: You Will be More Creative

When we look for new experiences, take in new ideas and learn new skills, it educates and inspires us. We broaden our horizons, begin to see things in new ways and think more creatively around challenges and obstacles. Instead of going for the safe option, we look at things in a new light and we find new energy. Stepping outside what is comfortable makes us bigger people, in every way. As human beings we need challenges; otherwise we stagnate.

Five: Your Comfort Zone Will Expand

The boundaries of your comfort zone are not fixed. They might be pretty narrow at the moment, but the more you push them, by trying new things, the wider they will become. The new things you try will become the norm and, eventually, part of your comfort zone. For instance, say you decide to start going for a half-hour walk three times a week. At first it's going to feel odd, you will feel like giving it a miss, argue with yourself that it doesn't really matter. But if you strengthen your resolve and do it, within two or three months your walk will be part of your regular routine, and therefore within your comfort zone – which in turn will have expanded. And that means that, knowing you can do something you set out to do, your self-belief and confidence will grow, and the next time you decide to make a change, you are far more likely to stick with it.

Stepping outside your comfort zone brings lasting benefits. You'll feel good about yourself, more able, sure of yourself and willing to try something new the next time. In other words, you feel more confident!

How Far Outside of the Zone Should I Step?

Pushing yourself to try something new or reach for the next level can have fantastic results. You may discover a side of yourself that you never knew and abilities that you haven't previously been aware of. But if you push too far it can all end in disaster. Push yourself beyond what is possible and you'll end up feeling bad, telling yourself you're a failure and that you should never have bothered trying. And that will put you off ever trying again.

Imagine your comfort zone as a circle. Around it is a bigger circle, often called the learning zone, then beyond that is an even bigger circle, known as the panic zone. When we reach the panic zone, we've pushed ourselves too far. So the goal is to push yourself beyond what is comfortable, but within the limits of what is manageable. It's about a controlled level of anxiety that you choose to let into your life by trying something new but achievable, rather than opening yourself up to sky-high anxiety that is out of control and will simply paralyse you.

We're all different. For one person, choosing to skydive is fun, a bit scary and a great challenge. For another person it's a truly horrific idea. What you want is to find challenges that bring out the best in you and spur you on to push yourself a bit further.

Take starting a new job, or learning to drive. At the start, both of these activities are pretty scary, but for most people they're manageable and we know that once we master them we're going to feel good. The first time you sit in a car and imagine handling the steering wheel, three different pedals and a gearstick all at once, it seems incredibly daunting. But stick with it and within a few hours you can manage the basics and see that you're going to get there. And that feels great.

The new job that you longed for can seem terrifying on your first day. You don't know your way around, or who is who, or what you're supposed to be doing. But you learn and the whole process is enjoyable, because we're at our best when we're learning something new.

Picking the Right Time

Uncertain times in our lives can also affect how we feel about making changes. When we're tired, down or ill, we are far more likely to want to stick with what we know. If things feel financially or socially precarious, then we're unlikely to want to push ourselves at that point. We may feel we already have enough to cope with.

It takes energy to make changes and to try new things. So while it's not a good idea to make excuses and keep putting something off (I really am going to take up exercise, just not this week), it's also wise to pick the right time, in order to give ourselves a better chance of succeeding.

Taking the First Steps

So we know that stepping outside our comfort zone is a good thing, but how do we go about it? What are the steps to take?

Start Slowly

Don't be afraid to start gently and slowly. There are no prizes for jumping right in with both feet and, no matter what the pace, in the end the benefits are likely to be the same. For instance, say you decide you are going to learn Spanish. You could enrol in an evening class three nights a week and then immerse yourself in CDs and videos for two hours every other night of the week. It would be demanding and probably exhausting, but if you had the willpower to stick with it you could end up speaking Spanish pretty quickly. Or you could take the evening class just one night a week and practise for an hour twice a week. You would learn more slowly, but you would still end up speaking Spanish, and the process wouldn't be quite so gruelling and full on.

Of course, you might start slowly and love it so much that you then decide to speed up and increase the intensity. But that's about growing enthusiasm, which is very different to hurling yourself at something. If you set off too hard and fast, it's much more likely you will fail, since that is what usually happens when you put impossible demands on yourself.

Do Everyday Things

Not all changes have to be big. You can make small changes in your everyday life that take you just a little way out of your comfort zone and help prepare you, essentially by letting you practise, for when the time comes to make bigger changes. You could start walking to the station each morning, instead of driving to work. You could give up meat or sugar for a month. If you work long hours, you could start leaving the office earlier once a week. You could cook a new dish every weekend, or set your alarm to get up earlier so that you have more quality time with your child, or you could start writing a journal. All of these kinds of changes are about expanding the parameters of what you do every day; you're pushing at the edges of your comfort zone, but not to the point where it hurts.

Make Decisions

Stepping outside your comfort zone is not just about doing practical things or activities, it's also about the way you choose to think. A great way of stretching your thought processes is to look at the way you make decisions. Do you hate pondering and tend to make snap decisions? If so, try deliberately slowing down the process, taking your time and really thinking about whatever choice you are making. On the other hand, if you take forever to make a decision, try speeding up and just picking one option straight away.

Neither way is wrong or right. Both can work, and both can lead to the wrong decision. But this is about looking at your habits, and trying a different way of doing things. Try it with small decisions first – cheese or ham for lunch, a drink with a friend or a quiet night in, that kind of thing.

Identify Your Fears

Stepping outside your comfort zone isn't just about trying new things, it's also about challenging your fears and overcoming them. There's no better feeling in the world, and no bigger confidence boost.

What is it that scares you? It might be some aspect of work, or perhaps something in your social life. Imagine there's someone you really fancy and you'd love to go out with them but are too afraid to ask. Overcoming your fear doesn't necessarily mean going straight up to them and suggesting a date. You could start by simply saying hello, smiling, or having a brief chat. Or imagine you've been asked to take on a new challenge at work and it feels pretty daunting. Instead of feeling overwhelmed and scared, remind yourself that you wouldn't have been asked if your boss didn't believe you could do it, and then work out what the first small step would be and concentrate on that.

Breaking out of your comfort zone and getting the better of your fears takes courage, and it really is fine to find that courage in stages.

Big Steps

Sometimes we do need to make a big move in order to challenge ourselves and step out of a suffocating, stuck-in-a-rut or negative situation into new territory. Maybe you've never travelled and you decide to go on the trip of a lifetime. Planning and preparing for it, researching the places you're going to and even learning a bit of the language might all be part of taking a big step out of your comfort zone.

Or perhaps you need to break out of a relationship that isn't bringing any benefits to your life and that may be making you unhappy or demoralised. It's not really possible to leave someone in small steps – yes, you can plan and prepare, but then you just have to go for it. Or perhaps you just feel stuck in your work, doing the same thing over and over, year after year. Time for a change – be brave, apply for all the jobs you think you might enjoy and then grasp any opportunity that comes your way.

If It All Goes Wrong

Stepping out of your comfort zone, however much it seems like the right thing and however carefully you plan and prepare, doesn't guarantee success. Sometimes things go wrong, and that's why taking a step forward is always a risk.

Of course it's much nicer if it goes right, especially first time. But the point is that, whether it goes right or wrong, what matters is that you found the courage to do it. And that's a success in itself. In stepping out of your comfort zone you pushed a mental block out of the way, you chose to see things differently, to do something different and to be someone braver and more hopeful than you were yesterday. If it did work, you will feel great. And if it didn't work, don't let it knock you back. Remind yourself that you were brave to try and make a decision to try it again, or try something else that tests you.

Josie, a girl I met a couple of years ago, was diagnosed with epilepsy when she was eighteen. She was just about to leave home for university when she had her first two fits. Josie was scared, and her parents were terrified. Intent on protecting her, they encouraged her to give up her university plans, get a safe job down the road and remain living at home.

For five years Josie did exactly that. She was put on medication for her epilepsy and found that it was largely under control, and she only suffered a handful of fits every year. But her parents still discouraged her from living independently.

Although Josie felt frustrated with her dead-end job, stifled by living with her parents and afraid that she wasn't using her brain, she accepted the situation until, in the summer of 2012, she watched the Paralympics and saw a band of extraordinary athletes overcome their disabilities and achieve amazing things. The cheering crowds, excited commentators and beaming medal winners weren't thinking about disability, they were too busy focusing on the achievement that discipline and determination had made into a reality.

Josie saw this and decided that she wasn't going to be held back by 'safe' boundaries any longer. She reapplied to university, got accepted and went to study 200 miles from home. In the summer of 2016, Josie graduated with a first-class history degree and, having decided to become a teacher, went on to complete her training.

Josie took the decision to step up, not down. She realised that she was the same person she had been before she developed epilepsy; the only thing that had changed was that she now had a condition she needed to manage. Her epilepsy could have limited her choices in life and stunted her confidence, but in the end she chose not to let it.

Josie's story reminded me that sometimes, with the best of intentions, the people around us hold us back. Josie's parents were afraid for her, that's why they wanted her to stay in the 'safe zone'. There are plenty of achievers who can remember someone saying, 'don't try that,' or 'you'll never manage it,' or 'why would you want to do that when you can stick with what you've got?' They may have a point, so don't instantly dismiss their words of warning, but if, in the end, you know that in order to be true to yourself you need to ignore well-meant advice and do the opposite, then trust your instincts and go for it.

Cracking the Catwalk

A fabulous story about comfort zones comes from a woman named Olivia Martin. Olivia was a medical student when she answered our advertisement for models to take part in the Ideal Home Show Diversity Catwalk. And she was just who we needed.

Olivia was, and is, gorgeous. But she'd been through a lot. Born with a heart condition known as Tetralogy of Fallot (TOF), she'd had a hole in her heart repaired during open-heart surgery at ten months old. Doctors warned her parents that she would need a second open-heart operation, probably by the age of five, but in fact Olivia remained healthy until she was twenty.

'The second surgery went really well, but my recovery was slow,' she says. 'My wound took a long time to close because a stitch that should have dissolved poked through, and I ended up with a keloid scar which is red, raised and itchy. I always assumed my second scar would be much like the first, which was barely noticeable and never itchy or painful, so I really struggled with this new, giant scar that was so sensitive I couldn't wear necklaces or woolly jumpers! As my health improved, I started wanting to exercise more to try to get my strength and stamina back, and my lovely friend Liz started taking me swimming. I soon stopped, though, as I felt sure everyone at the pool was staring at my chest and talking about me. I covered up my scar with high-neck t-shirts and scarves and gave away my favourite low-neckline clothes.

'I've never been a fashionista, but I'd always enjoyed pretty clothes and hated wearing dull clothes to hide my scar. Even so, I carried on like that for quite some time. My friends and family and my boyfriend were all loving and supportive and told me that the scar didn't matter, but I was afraid to show it, convinced that anyone looking at me would be horrified by it. I guess I was horrified by it myself.

'Then I read a post on Facebook by a girl with a similar scar, saying that she didn't know where to find a bikini to cover her scar for a girlie holiday and she was worried about whether or not to go. There was an outpouring of support for her, and encouragement to show her scar and be proud.

'I was about to go on holiday to Crete with my fiancé. So I decided that, rather than covering up, which I had been planning to do, I would set an example and show others with scars that you needn't be afraid. So I swallowed my fear and asked my boyfriend to take a photo of me on the beach in a cute bikini with my scar out for all to see. It was a huge step out of my comfort zone, but when the time came I was actually far more embarrassed about posing on a packed beach than I was about my scar.

'Somehow that day, things shifted for me. No one stared or criticised or even commented. Some people glanced at me, but they just looked curious, they weren't judging me. After that, I stopped covering my scar. I went back to wearing low tops and binned all the scarves and high-neck tops. The spell was broken. I still had off days when I felt it stood out a mile, but they were fewer and fewer as time went on.

'Then I saw the ad for the diversity show. On an impulse I sent off the beach photo. I forgot about it until I received an email saying I had been chosen. I was thrilled, but taking part in the show definitely took me out of my comfort zone again. We had two rehearsals and fittings, and then we did three shows a day for three days. During the first day of rehearsals we were asked if we would be willing to do a swimwear finale. I looked awkwardly at my feet. Realising my hesitation, the incredible stylist that Katie had chosen for us reassured me that he wouldn't let any of us go out in something we weren't comfortable in. I nervously agreed to go out in swimwear, trying not to think about it too much.

'The first show rolled around extremely quickly and as we lined up backstage waiting for our cue, I realised I was shaking like a leaf. I have never been so nervous in all my life. I started to worry about what people would think, say, and post online! Stepping onto the catwalk, I was shocked at how many people had turned up. There wasn't even room to stand, and at the end there was a bank of flashing cameras. The sheer shock and confusion on my face must have been hilarious! I think the audience could sense my nerves and, as I walked down the catwalk, they cheered me on. I made it to the end of the stage and back without falling over and felt as good as if I had won the lottery!

'After that first show, the rest were so much fun. All of us models had a great time backstage, getting to know each other and messing around. The make-up artists let me take photos at each stage, since I am useless at all things girlie, because I was determined to try the make-up at home. Loads of my friends and family came to see and support me, and I got to meet the other girls' families, too.

'Walking round the Ideal Home Show between shows, people stopped us to say "Well done", or tell us their stories and even show us their scars. Suddenly, I wanted to get my scar out rather than hide it in high-necked tops! By the last day, far from being nervous, I was struggling not to have a little dance to the music while I was on stage in my bikini.

'Being a part of the show was wonderful. I am getting married soon, and I had been dreading dress shopping because there aren't many options for a dress that would cover up my scar. But after the show I decided to go for the dress that I wanted, with a sweetheart neckline and plenty of lace.

'Now I go swimming with my friends when the weather is nice and I wear the gorgeous bikini I wore on the catwalk. And best of all, I have made friends for life with a bunch of strong, beautiful, inspirational women who taught me that it doesn't matter that you appear different. Beautiful is about so much more than how you look.

'I am finally proud of what I went through, and I know that without my scar I could never be where I am today: getting married to an amazing man, qualified as a doctor, and blessed with friends and family who support me through everything.'

What an inspiring story. Olivia didn't just take a big step outside her comfort zone once, she did it twice. The courage she found in putting on a bikini and posing on the beach led her to come along and strut her stuff on the catwalk at the show. Her comfort zone had expanded, and then it expanded again. And with it, her confidence.

So if you're in doubt about stepping out of your comfort zone, don't be. I hope this chapter has helped you to see that even making that first step - no matter how big or small - will bring you rewards and give your confidence an amazing boost.

CHAPTER

Making Mistakes

We all make mistakes. We are all human and messing up occasionally comes with the job description. The trouble is, when we do get it wrong, we tend to give ourselves a hard time about it. There's nothing worse than that sinking feeling when you realise you've made a miscalculation, offended someone, been conned or messed up in some way. That's when we start to feel ashamed, guilty and self-blaming.

I've made loads of mistakes: small ones, big ones, work ones, personal ones – I could write a very long list. And I do tend to get tough on myself about them. In fact, I've even taken on imaginary mistakes sometimes, telling myself that I was to blame for something when actually I wasn't.

Like so many people, I always felt it was not OK to make mistakes, that I should somehow always get things right, and if I didn't, I was a failure. But then I realised, thanks to advice from a few wise and trusted people, that if you aren't making mistakes, then you aren't really living. Life is full of situations where you get to try new things, meet new people and experiment, so of course we're going to get it wrong sometimes. And when we do, we can choose whether to disappear into a vat of self-blame or forgive ourselves, learn from our mistakes and move on.

The funny thing is that, while we hate to make mistakes ourselves, we love hearing about other people's mistakes! Perhaps that's because it gives us permission to make mistakes, too. We love TV programmes in which the characters mess up and then mess up again and struggle to put things right. Take Ellie, the character played by Olivia Colman in *Broadchurch*. She was always making mistakes (like not realising that her husband was a murderer!) and becoming tearful. But ultimately she was a strong woman who got a grip on things, solved problems and put her life back together.

If you let it, the fear of getting things wrong, of messing up and making mistakes, can paralyse you. On the other hand, if you're prepared to accept that you *will* make mistakes and it doesn't make you a bad person, then you can live life to the full.

Knowing how to handle the situation when you make mistakes is a vital tool in the confidence toolbox. A mistake can dent or even destroy your confidence – or it can help your confidence grow. It all depends on how you deal with it.

What are Mistakes?

Sounds like a silly question, doesn't it? But actually it's a good idea to start off by being really clear about what a mistake is and why it's impossible not to make mistakes just about every day of your life.

We've got a lot of words for mistake – error, blunder, fault, omis-

sion, miscalculation, gaffe, oversight, faux pas, misconception . . .
I could go on and on. The point is, it's something we're all very
familiar with. We have so many names for mistakes because they
are a common occurrence – they happen every day.

Essentially, a mistake is an action or decision that we come to
regret because of the consequences for ourselves and for others –
which might be anything from a missed train to a broken heart. A
mistake isn't the same as an accident. An accident is unavoidable;
it's not planned, it simply happens. A mistake is usually something
we have done consciously and intentionally because we think
it is all right, until it leads to trouble. An accident is simply an
accident, whereas a mistake only becomes one when you realise
it afterwards. A dropped plate is an accident; making a mean
comment is a mistake.

A mistake is a wrong decision. It can, sometimes, lead to an
accident, but it's not the same thing. Neither is it the same thing
as a failure. Trying something and failing, tough as that can be,
is not a mistake. If you run a race and lose, or send your book
to a publisher and get a rejection, or put in for a promotion and
don't get it, that's a failure rather than a mistake. Failure hurts, and
we need to get back up and try again (it's worth bearing in mind
that almost all great successes come on the back of a good few
failures that took place first!) but mistakes are not about trying
and failing, they're about something going wrong.

There are so many different kinds of mistakes, ranging from
very minor to enormous. Mostly they're small – getting a parking
ticket, buying a dress or shirt that you thought you'd grow to like
and then didn't, painting your bedroom red because it seemed
like a good idea at the time, putting an embarrassing photo on

Instagram, repeating a small bit of gossip you were asked to keep private, forgetting to set your alarm clock, and so on.

Small mistakes aren't so bad, we all make them every day and generally there aren't any terrible consequences. We can double-check the parking or the alarm next time, give the dress/shirt away, promise ourselves not to do any more gossiping and make better photo choices.

After that come bigger mistakes. Walking out of a good job in a huff; walking out of a relationship in a huff; getting drawn into a damaging relationship; saying no to a great opportunity; missing a crucial exam; borrowing money you can't pay back.

The thing about a mistake is that it feels OK, or even quite good, at the time – it's only afterwards that you regret it. Sometimes we do know or sense that we're making a mistake, but much more often we don't. It seems like the right thing to do; we're pretty sure we're right; we need to be free of the job or the relationship; we can't help falling in love (and ignoring the signs that someone might be unstable); the great opportunity seems like too big a risk; we imagine we'll never need that exam; and we're certain we'll be able to pay back the money. It's only when we're unemployed, broken-hearted, hurt, regretful about the missed opportunity, or broke and struggling to repay a debt that we realise that our action was a mistake.

Fear of Mistakes

The fear of getting something wrong, of making a mistake and messing up, is pretty big for most of us, because when we get something wrong it makes us feel that there's something wrong with *us*. So we try to avoid it, or to cover it up, hide it, ignore it. We don't grow up learning to say 'I don't know,' or 'I could be wrong'. We think we need to be right.

Most of us were brought up to think that making a mistake was a bad thing. In school we tried not to make mistakes in our work – a mistake meant a bad mark. And later that transferred to work and to life. Get it wrong and you're marked down.

The thing is, a mistake can often lead to a breakthrough. In science, in discoveries, in developing new ways to do things, people have always made mistakes before they worked out how to do something. Mistakes are part of a learning curve – innovation flourishes in an environment where it's all right to make mistakes. And that's true for us in life, too. When we make mistakes it can be a chance to learn. It doesn't always mean that we're incompetent; it sometimes means that we're trying, even if we fail. Don't forget that even the most successful people have made mistakes – in fact, they're usually the ones who made more mistakes than the rest of us, but who weren't afraid to get it wrong and try again.

When It Isn't Your Fault

Before we start talking about how to cope with mistakes, we need to be sure that a mistake was actually ours. It's easy to blame ourselves for something that wasn't truly our fault.

After I was attacked, in all my pain, confusion and shame, I felt that I had made a huge mistake in choosing to go out with a man who ended up raping me and then arranging to have acid thrown at me. I questioned my judgement and asked myself why

I hadn't picked up on the signs, why I had allowed myself to end up in that situation.

It took me a long time to understand that I wasn't at fault. I had accepted a date with someone who seemed nice and who concealed who he actually was. He could have turned out to be a decent guy, but he didn't. It was unfortunate and not my mistake. So take a good look at the situation and make sure that you're not blaming yourself for something that wasn't your fault.

So What Do We Do?

The mistake has been made. There's no undoing it, you feel awful, you keep telling yourself how stupid you are and you wish desperately that you could turn back time and have another chance. You imagine that life will never be the same, you blame yourself, go over and over what happened, and in your imagination you spot all the opportunities you had to change your mind or do it differently. You feel as though you're the only person who's ever made this particular mistake, and you're pretty sure it's the biggest mistake ever made.

You can run this cycle round in your head over and over again, as you slump under the duvet certain you can never show your face again. But you can't let your mistakes define your life. So when you reach the point where you'd like to get past this mistake, however humongous it was, and move on, there are three stages which will help you:

- **Take Responsibility**
- **Learn from It**
- **Forgive Yourself**

Take Responsibility

Taking responsibility for your mistakes isn't the same as brooding over them. That will only leave you feeling miserable, helpless and stuck. Taking responsibility means owning up, even if it's only to yourself. Admitting 'I got it wrong' is not so terrible when you realise that we all get things wrong. Not one of us is perfect or immune to doing the wrong thing.

Once you've owned the mistake, without making excuses or blaming someone else, then look at whether it's possible to put it right, or at least apologise. Doing whatever you can to repair the situation is not only the right thing to do, it's also vital if you're going to get past the mistake and move on.

Consider what you might do. If you owe money, arrange to pay it back, even if you can't pay much at a time. You might be able to find extra income from a second job, or save money by altering your lifestyle. Debts can be a huge burden, so it's worth making the extra effort to free yourself from it. And if the debt is to a friend or family member, you'll want to save the relationship, too.

If you've hurt someone, apologise. Whatever you did, a genuine, heartfelt apology will usually help. If you can't talk to the person, put your apology in writing – a letter or card is better than an email – and make sure they get it. You could send flowers or a gift, too, but it's the words you use in apologising that will mean the most.

Saying sorry and doing what you can to put things right will help you to move on. But what about situations where we have made mistakes which we deeply regret, but which we can't put right? What if you feel that you were unkind to someone who has since died? Or if you've ended a relationship in a way that you regret, ignoring the other person's feelings?

It can help our happiness levels if we 'pay' for these errors in some way.

It's no accident that in some religions there is an accepted procedure for facing wrongdoings, confessing them, asking for forgiveness and accepting some penitential task as a means of atoning for them. But I believe that everyone, religious or not, can find peace within themselves if they try to put their mistakes right in some appropriate way. If someone you would like to apologise to has died, you could lay flowers for them or light a candle. Or if a relationship has ended acrimoniously, you could write a letter to your former partner, thanking them for the happier times you once shared.

Doing something, even when the person you want to apologise to isn't around, will ease your bruised spirit and help you to think of them more peacefully.

Whatever your mistake, there will be something that you can do towards putting it right.

Most mistakes, enormous as they can seem, don't ruin your life. Even something as big as marrying the wrong person, stealing from your employer, running off with your best friend's boyfriend or having a huge tattoo that you later hate, may not seem so terrible a few years down the line. We're programmed to get over things, and we do. We even laugh about them, hard as that is to imagine when the misery of your mistake is fresh and raw.

When you've done all you can to atone for your mistake, give yourself permission to take your mind off it. Do something you enjoy, listen to music, watch a film, see friends, let yourself move on and recognise that dealing with mistakes is part of life.

Luckily most mistakes are forgotten. Pain doesn't last forever. We live to move on, realise that it's OK to be happy again and laugh at ourselves.

Learn From It

Is there a lesson you can learn from your mistake? If so, make sure you recognise the value in it. Hopefully you won't make the same mistake again. My worst mistakes have taught me some of life's most important lessons.

It's worth reflecting on what happened before and during the mistake. What could you have done differently? Were you rushing (speed, whether on the road or anywhere else, leads to a lot of mistakes)? Were you distracted, or trying to fit too much into your day? Is there anything you can take from it that would be useful?

I know that in my own life I've done all kinds of things wrong, and each time I try to learn from it. Getting things right can take practice, and making mistakes along the way is inevitable.

Our mistakes help us grow – if we're willing to learn from them. We discover what to do, what *not* to do, and better ways to approach problems or relationships.

For example, if you've lost your job due to a mistake you made, then there may not be much you can do to put it right, but you can definitely learn from it. And that may be something that a future boss will appreciate about you.

Whenever I'm rushing from one place to the next (which for me is far too often) I think of this story:

A television news reporter I know, Sue (not her real name), told me about a mistake which still makes her blush ten years later.

She had been sent out by her boss to cover a heart-warming

story which was to go out live that evening on the programme she worked for. It was about a disabled boy whose family were determined to take him to Disney World. His parents and the local community had come up with all sorts of exciting and innovative ways of raising money for the trip, and they had nearly reached their target.

Sue set about recording comments from a range of local people, and she made sure that the cameraman got some lovely footage of the child playing with his dog. She then interviewed the little boy's parents – who were lively and fun. She was running late now to complete the job in time, but just before she left to go back to the studio, she double-checked the parents' surname and made sure that she had the correct spelling for the onscreen caption that would accompany her story later.

Unfortunately, what she didn't do was check the *child's* surname. And – as sometimes happens – his mother had remarried and she and her new husband had a different surname from her son.

When Sue recorded the voiceover for her report, she used the wrong surname for the boy. That was bad enough, but in some of the film footage, you could see fundraising posters dotted around the place, which of course had the child's *correct* surname on them. In her haste to get the report on air in time, Sue didn't notice her mistake.

After the news programme, she bumped into her boss in the corridor. He looked her up and down in fury and yelled: 'You got the kid's name wrong. That was unforgiveable!' And he stormed off.

Sue cried herself to sleep that night. She was mortified at having made the mistake and worried that she was in the wrong job and might never succeed in her career. As it happens, she went on to become very successful. 'Still,' she says, 'I never, ever got anyone's name wrong again! In fact, I became almost obsessive about checking details. And that's no bad thing for a reporter.'

Forgive Yourself

While it's important to take responsibility when you make a mistake, to put right what you can and to learn from it, it's also important to forgive yourself.

If you've made a mistake that has impacted on the happiness of others, or that has changed your life in some painful way, then you may be left with a mountain of guilt and regret. But while you can't alter the past, you *can* change how you think about it.

Going over and over your mistake, punishing yourself, blaming yourself and feeling that you're a terrible person won't help. It will make you miserable and will probably make you pretty hard to be around, too. Extending some compassion towards yourself for being human is not the same as saying the mistake doesn't matter. It's about showing yourself a little understanding, realising that you're not perfect and that you'll probably make other mistakes in the future. If you can forgive yourself, you can forgive others. And let's face it: the world needs a bit more forgiveness.

Do you need a good reason to forgive yourself? Here are three:

One – you didn't make the mistake on purpose

You didn't set out with the intention of getting something wrong or causing harm. The very nature of a mistake is that it was unintentional. Or at least the outcome was unintentional. You meant well; it was not an act of malice or unkindness, it was an error. You misunderstood something, miscalculated, rushed or made the wrong decision, but you didn't intend to cause anyone a problem or unhappiness. You didn't deliberately create a calamity, so forgive yourself, because whatever happened, it doesn't mean you're a bad person, just a mistaken one.

TWO – YOU WOULD FORGIVE SOMEONE ELSE

Most of us are harder on ourselves than we are on others, so it's a lot easier to forgive someone else for a mistake than it is to forgive ourselves. Try to imagine what your reaction would be if your friend, partner or fellow worker had done what you did. How long would you stay angry? Would you be angry at all, or would you understand?

If you would readily forgive another person for the same mistake you made, why are you having a hard time forgiving yourself? Don't you deserve the same understanding as anyone else? Being tough on ourselves can be a hard habit to break; it's as though we think that if we show ourselves even a tiny bit of niceness then it's self-indulgent and will make us a failure. But actually the bigger failure is refusing to be forgiving towards yourself. We know that treating children with love makes them more confident and successful. It's the same with ourselves.

THREE – THERE WILL BE A NEXT TIME

This one's certain. You will mess up again. We all will. So you might as well work out a way of dealing with your mistakes that doesn't leave you full of shame and guilt. Because, however big or small each mistake we make, we have to carry on. And if you agonise over every mistake and make yourself feel terrible, you're not going to be able to function well in the world. You can't expect yourself to be infallible or mistake-proof, and you can't get in a complete stew over every mistake. You need to forgive yourself so that you can learn to be resilient and flexible around mistakes, to accept your responsibility, be able to sort out the situation and move on.

I'm not advocating being flippant if the mistake is pretty serious, but it's worth developing a 'you win some, you lose some' attitude which will help keep you buoyant in tough times.

There's a great story about forgiveness that always makes me smile. It's about Warren Buffett, the American billionaire investor and philanthropist. Now in his eighties, Warren Buffett is the chairman of Berkshire Hathaway, a hugely successful investment company. According to a report, a few years back one of the company's senior managers came to Mr Buffett and told him, nervously, that a project he was overseeing had gone sour and had lost the company a lot of money. He expected to be fired, so imagine his amazement when Mr Buffett said to him, 'We all make mistakes. If you don't make mistakes, you can't make decisions.' Mr Buffett also pointed out that he had made bigger mistakes himself.

In treating the situation this way, Warren Buffett won the respect and loyalty of the manager, who would almost certainly never make such a mistake again. If only all bosses were like this. Sadly they're not, but even if the outcome isn't so positive, don't treat a mistake as though it's the end of the world.

Use Humour

If you're struggling to forgive yourself for your mistakes, laughter can help. American writer William Arthur Ward said, 'To make mistakes is human; to stumble is commonplace; to be able to laugh at yourself is maturity.' That sums it up pretty well. Laughter is like a magic potion: it soothes tension, lifts your mood and makes everything seem just that bit easier.

I know you may not feel like laughing – the misery, embarrassment and pain may be too fresh – but laughter will help you forget about your mistake faster than anything else can.

It takes courage to see the funny side, but there usually is one. So once you've dealt with the serious side, the next step is to laugh about it.

Moving On

When we make a big mistake it really can feel like the end of the world. But it isn't; life goes on and we recover.

I recently came across a man who ten years earlier thought his world had ended. He made a huge mistake at work: while working crazy hours and feeling under enormous pressure, he fixed the books to make the sums add up. He didn't steal, but he committed fraud and as a result he was sacked. With that on his record, he couldn't get another job. His marriage was put under strain and eventually his wife left him, telling him he was impossible to be around. Then he discovered he had bowel cancer, perhaps in part due to all the stress. He'd been eating badly, drinking too much, taking too many sleeping pills and not looking after himself. At that point he believed his life could only go downhill. He had made a big mistake and he'd paid for it with his job, his marriage and his health. But he survived the cancer and today he's in a job that makes him much happier and he's remarried with two small daughters. Would he have believed all this to be possible? No, but somehow he kept going and, as he told me, somewhere along the way he forgave himself and vowed to start again. He really did grow and learn from his mistakes.

If you're at a point where you feel everything is falling apart because of a particular thing you did, please don't despair. Breathe deeply, get a pencil and a piece of paper, and make a plan to start rebuilding your life, one small step at a time. If you've lost your job, you could apply for five new jobs, sending out your CVs to all of them and doing three follow-up calls to different potential employers each day. Taking action makes us feel better, and also helps to shift us when we're stuck, not to mention helping others see that we really do want to fix our mistakes.

One thing that has really helped me over the years is writing things down in a journal. Especially when you don't want to burden others, you can offload your deepest, darkest thoughts with a pen and paper. It's private and – if you want to – you can simply destroy it the next day. The process of spilling your feelings onto the page really does ease the burden.

I hope to teach my daughter that making mistakes is OK, it's part of life and no one should feel terrible over something that they've done wrong. I want her to know that life is all about choices, and sometimes we make the wrong one, and it hurts. We feel awful and we have to deal with the consequences. But we shouldn't define ourselves by our mistakes. In moving on from a mistake, you can find new strength and productive energy. Accept it; put right what you can; forgive yourself and do your best to learn from it.

Then let it go, and get on with the rest of your life.

Live with Purpose

We're here, living life, whether we want to be or not. And whether it feels like a good day or a bad one, we still have to get up and put one foot in front of the other. For me, having purpose to my life and meaningful goals for each day gives me a reason to keep moving forward, as well as a way to measure how far I've come and motivate myself to keep going when things get tough. You can't choose all the outcomes in life, but you can choose the direction you go in. Decide who you want to be, and what you want to achieve, then take charge of it. Without that, you're just letting life 'happen', floating along waiting for chance to decide where you end up. And that isn't the route to feeling fulfilled, happy and confident.

We all need a sense of purpose, and we all want our life to have meaning. In fact, it's well established that a sense of purpose is necessary for psychological health. Without it, we're lost, directionless and prone to depression. If you think back through history to our beginnings, human evolution depends on motivation, our will to survive and our feeling that life remains worth the effort.

With purpose and meaning essential to our health, we can't help but automatically look for them. And we find them in all kinds of places. They aren't rare; both are very present in our lives. We find meaning in relationships, in connections with friends and family, in our work and studies, in our search for enlightenment or fulfilment, and in making our own contribution to society.

But sometimes, when difficult things happen, purpose and meaning can feel in short supply and we find ourselves adrift. When this happens, when we lose our bearings, confidence seeps away and so does our sense of direction in life. That certainly happened to me, and I know many others who, for any number of reasons, have found themselves wondering, 'What is my purpose?' 'What should I be doing now?' 'How do I get back out there and deal with life when suddenly it all seems so hard?'

I know, from my own experience and from those of others, that it is always possible to find meaning and purpose, even when life has dealt you the most severe of blows. And I know, too, that, as you rediscover a sense of purpose and meaning in your day-to-day life, your confidence naturally blossoms.

What is Purpose?

When we do something with purpose, we do it intentionally, with the aim of a certain outcome. To live purposefully is to work towards achieving goals we have set for ourselves and to generate results that we feel matter, whether these are practical or material.

If you are looking for purpose, you are fundamentally saying, 'What can I do with my time that is worthwhile?'

What is worthwhile will be different for each of us, depending on our outlook, talents, abilities and interests. So for one person it might be cooking a delicious meal, for another it's working with children, for another it's a job in the media and for another it's driving a bus. It doesn't matter what it is that you do, as long as it has meaning for you. Because when we do things and achieve things and master new skills, it raises our self-esteem and our confidence.

This isn't necessarily about proving ourselves, or about competition with others. Your purpose might be to paint, or to create a garden, or to learn to meditate. The self-esteem boost comes from following through on your intention, learning as you do so, and ultimately achieving your goal.

When we act with purpose we are proving something to ourselves. Whether you set out to be a polar explorer or to go for a half-hour walk three times a week, if you follow through with it you will feel a wonderful sense of achievement. You will know that you can trust yourself to see your goals through and that will make you have confidence in yourself.

Purpose can – and should – apply to every part of your life. We often think of purpose as something that primarily comes into play at work, but actually it's far more than that. We can set ourselves goals in our relationships and friendships in the way we care for ourselves, in our hobbies and interests, in personal challenges and when it comes to how we treat strangers.

To act with purpose is to take responsibility for setting our own goals and then take action to achieve them.

Your Purpose

Sometimes, especially when life is feeling difficult, it can be hard to think about purpose. Just getting through each day can be hard enough. At times like this, it can help to ask yourself a few questions:

Am I satisfied with the job I have – and if so, what do I want to achieve?

If I don't currently have a job, what five skills can I offer an employer?

How important is work to me, compared to other things in life?

How much of my time am I willing to spend at work?

Where would I like my career to be in five years' time?

Am I satisfied with my partner and relationship?

If not, what changes do I need to make?

Do I want to marry, and if so, why?

Do I want children?

What qualities do I want in a partner?

What do I have to offer a partner?

Am I healthy? If not, what do I need to do to improve my health?

Do I have deep and satisfying friendships?

Are my finances well organised and under control?

What do I do in life that I love?

Is my life in balance?

The answers to these questions will give you an idea of where to start in setting yourself goals and moving forward meaningfully in your life. Don't feel you have to make goals huge and impressive; keep them small, especially if you are finding life tough at the moment. You might aim for something as simple as having a cup of tea with a friend, reading a book or tidying out a cupboard. These things, done with intention, will move you forward towards other goals, and will increase your self-esteem and confidence as you clock up each success.

How I Found Purpose

In the first few months after the attack I was absolutely at rock bottom. I was at the point where I seriously doubted my ability to ever recover mentally. Physically I was mending, very slowly, but I felt so low that I couldn't envisage any future for myself at all. I had only ventured out of my parents' house a handful of times, when I had been stared at, called a freak and a monster, and had had someone yell at me, 'Get out of my shop.'

When the idea of making a documentary was first mentioned to me, by some journalists I met through my wonderful surgeon, Mr Jawad, I had to think long and hard. I felt such shame and embarrassment about being raped and I was still in a lot of pain – would going public about what had happened to me make it worse, or even put me in danger? I would lose my anonymity. But set against that was the possibility of bringing hope to other victims. My treatment and rehabilitation had been pioneering, and I wanted people to know about it. I thought perhaps it might give people insight into what had happened to me.

At that point I had no idea what to do with my life. I had no job and I was bored and lost. As I was a trained beautician I had wondered if I could train to do tattooing for burns and cancer victims, but I couldn't even afford a college course, now that I was on disability benefit.

Saying yes to the documentary was an incredibly hard decision, but I felt I had nothing to lose and no other way forward. Right up to the moment the documentary was aired on Channel 4, I felt terrified. Would anyone even watch? And if they did, how would people respond?

When the producer got in touch to say there had been 3.8 million viewers, I was totally stunned. At first I thought she was telling me there had been that many complaints! The response was extraordinary. It seemed the whole world responded. I had letters and emails, and people stopped me in the street, almost all of them telling me how brave I was and expressing support. I was invited to go to the USA, Australia and Europe and asked about interviews and books.

It was heartening and encouraging. Suddenly I didn't feel so alone, and when I decided to set up a charity to help others in my situation a future began to open up for me.

I still had no money, so at first it was just me and a phone, working for free, seven days a week. But now I had a goal and I had purpose, and that gave me the courage and confidence to approach people for advice and support as I gradually built up the Katie Piper Foundation to what it is today: a thriving organisation with offices, two full-time staff, a board of voluntary trustees as well as supporters who give their time so generously because they believe in us and the work we are doing.

As well as a whole range of workshops and treatments for burns survivors, we give funding to enable people to travel to specialist treatments centres abroad like the one I went to in France. One of my biggest long-term goals is to be able to set up a similar centre in the UK. We also have an academic journal called *Scars, Burns & Healing* in which healthcare professionals report on cases and evidence so that we can help move treatments forward. We offer mentoring and run an annual academic course called Scar Academy, to which we invite European speakers so they can share new or pioneering techniques and methods of treatment.

It took a leap in the dark to find my purpose. I had to step way out of my comfort zone and agree to be filmed at a time when I could barely even look in the mirror. And as with any leap in the dark, it could have gone horribly wrong. Instead, I discovered just how generous and warm people can be, and I found a new direction in life – one I had never expected.

I worked incredibly hard to build the Foundation, and I continue to work hard to keep it going. I never forget the days when I felt there was no one to turn to for professional support or advice. One of my goals is to provide a source of support so that no one else has to go through that.

One of the decisions I made early on was that there was no point in feeling sorry for myself or moaning about my situation for the rest of my life. I could have stayed angry, bitter and sorry for myself, but if I had, I might as well not have lived. I felt that I'd survived for a reason, and my sense of purpose, when I found it, helped to keep me going and keep me strong.

Finding purpose can give you enormous strength, courage and confidence. Once I'd resolved that my purpose was to help others,

I found the confidence to approach donors to ask for help and advice, which I'd never have managed if it had been just about me. Having purpose also taught me a huge amount. In the early days I had no idea how to delegate, or when to stop because I was exhausted. I had to learn how to manage myself and how to work with other people, delegating, trusting and accepting support.

Today I'm so proud of the Foundation and of the work it does. I still have to pinch myself sometimes when I think that I've been part of creating something that helps people in the same position I was once in, those who feel that life as they knew it has ended and have no idea what comes next. It gives me purpose every day and, along with my husband and daughter, this shapes my life.

Finding Your Purpose

If you feel that your life, or one particular area of your life, is without purpose, I promise you that these few tips that I learned will really help.

One: Take Action

You might be wondering how you can take action if you don't know what it is that you want to do. Sometimes you can't *think up* your purpose, so you have to actually *do* things to try to find your way in. Taking action can produce results that endless hours of thinking just can't. For instance, I had a friend, Mac, who felt very lost and couldn't decide what to do after he was made redundant from his office job. He loved swimming, so his partner encouraged him to go and swim every day, just to fill some of the hours that he was spending sitting around fretting about jobs. Reluctantly, he did go swimming. It made him feel better, so he swam some more. And then one day it came to him – what did he love? What filled him with passion and energy and confidence? Swimming! So he decided he would become a swimming instructor. He qualified and started teaching, then he set up a local swimming club and soon he was coaching a squad that reached the national finals. He had never been so happy.

I'm not saying it would be that straightforward for all of us, but doing something constructive and worthwhile – whether that's exercise of some sort, voluntary work or a pursuit that interests you –will simultaneously develop your confidence as well as your sense of purpose.

Two: Let Go of The Ideal

Sometimes we keep ourselves stuck by hanging onto the idea that the outcome has to be completely right; it has to be THE ONE THING that you know you were meant to be doing, the thing that will change your life.

But there isn't just one purpose that's right for you, there are many that are potentially right for you. So pick one and get going. Another friend of mine decided she wanted to be a plumber. She trained and started work, but although she was a good plumber, she soon realised that this wasn't it – plumbing didn't give her any sense of purpose, it simply passed the days. Her boss loved being a plumber; she had found her niche and set up a successful company, but my friend felt something else was still out there for her. Step forward photography. She had always loved taking pictures for fun, but then she won a photographic competition and that was it – she apprenticed herself to a successful studio photographer, taking a big salary drop to do so, and set about learning the ropes until she knew enough to work on her own. Today she's a very good, in-demand photographer with a busy career, and this time she really has found what gives her life purpose.

Three: Let Go of What You Don't Want

It helps not just to look for your purpose but also to let go of those things that bring you no happiness and no sense of achievement. What is there in your life that drags you down, uses up your energy and feels joyless? It might be a job, a relationship or something you do out of a sense of obligation or habit. Sometimes you find that you've outgrown something you once enjoyed, or that you're doing something you don't actually need to do, just because you think you should. Someone I know recently told me that they had taken the decision to let go of a friendship that had become incredibly draining and one-sided. Another person I know had worked as a school governor for ten years and realised it was time to stop. She had loved it and worked very hard to help the school, but her kids had long since left and the school was taking up all her spare time.

If you're ending something, do it with kindness and goodwill and avoid hurting others where possible. Then move on and start to enjoy the space you've opened up in your life.

Four: When Are You Happiest?

Think about those times when you are at your happiest – and by that I mean so absorbed that you don't notice time pass. The activities that have this effect are different for all of us and often they can lead us towards finding purpose in life. It could be anything

– fishing, cooking, drawing, playing music, writing, entertaining children or any one of a thousand other things. Look at Nadiya Hussain, winner of *The Great British Bake Off* in 2015. She loved making cakes for her family, and it led her to apply to go on the show – and then to victory and a whole new career as a cook and celebrity. Nadiya is a wonderful example of someone who overcame self-doubt and lack of confidence. She was almost too scared to go on *Bake Off* at all, but she forced herself to step out of her comfort zone and do it, and with each week of the show her confidence grew.

Think about what you love doing so much that it makes time fly, and then do it, often and with real pleasure. You never know what may come out of it.

Five: Do Something for Others

If you really have no idea which way is forward for you and life seems grim, then break the cycle of despondency by doing something for other people. You'll not only be helping others, you'll be taking your mind off yourself, and that can be hugely beneficial.

There are dozens of worthy voluntary projects going on in every area, and it's great to get involved with something where you'll meet new people with whom you can work. I met a guy who got involved in cleaning up the beach near his home and ended up learning to surf. It gave him a spare-time passion that took him to surf spots all over the world and gave him real joy. A woman I know started volunteering to put together parcels for children in Romanian orphanages and through it she met her future husband. Volunteering is good for you, good for others, it's sociable and it creates a sense of purpose. So if you're stuck, choose something – anything – and give it a try.

Puppy Love

I first met Jamie Pound a few years back and we immediately got on well. Jamie is bright, funny and good company. We met because Jamie had been burned over 45 per cent of his body after an electrical fire. In 2010 he was 22 and a newly qualified electrician when he was working with a team rewiring a local college. Jamie was asked to test a cable, but someone in the team had forgotten to switch the power off. There was an explosion and Jamie's t-shirt was set on fire, burning his chest, arms, hands and head.

After being airlifted to hospital, Jamie was put in an induced coma for 15 days while grafts were taken from his legs and back to treat the burns. It was six weeks before he left hospital and over the next 18 months there were more operations and a tough regime of physiotherapy.

A few months into his recovery, Jamie split up with his long-term girlfriend. 'I didn't blame her,' he says. 'It was a lot to cope with; I was in bandages and constantly having dressings changed and treatments. I wasn't the guy she'd known before.'

With no job and no girlfriend, Jamie felt lost. 'I was at home watching TV all day and thinking, what am I going to do?' Jamie says. 'I'd loved being an electrician, I'd worked for it through a four-year apprenticeship, but I couldn't go back to it. I'd loved playing football with my mates, but I couldn't do that either. I'd go along and watch, but I didn't feel part of it anymore. My confidence had taken a huge knock and I had no idea what to do next.'

Jamie put all his efforts into getting better. 'I treated it like a job,' he says. 'I'd get up in the morning and go to the gym, have a physio session, eat a healthy meal and then go for a walk. I made myself do a nine-to-five day just concentrating on recovering. There were days when I pulled a sickie because I couldn't face going out of the house, but I kept going.'

For a long time that in itself was Jamie's purpose. But as he got stronger and his injuries healed, he needed a new purpose. Then Jamie was given a puppy, a German Shepherd he called Frankie. Jamie adored him, and took him along to a local dog-training class.

'It wasn't very good,' he says. 'So I looked for something else and found a dog trainer called Steve Mann. I went to one of his classes and thought he was brilliant so I signed up for a course.'

It was there that Jamie met Gemma, a veterinary nurse who was also on the course because she did a lot of dog walking and wanted to learn some training techniques. Jamie and Gemma hit it off and soon began seeing one another. Then, encouraged by Steve, Jamie decided he would train as a dog trainer. He qualified in November 2012 and a few months later he moved in with Gemma and her small daughter, Gracie.

Just before Christmas 2015, Jamie and Gemma got married. I went to their wedding and I couldn't have been happier for them. Now they've got two children, three dogs and their own very successful dog-training business in Chorleywood, Hertfordshire. It's not the future Jamie imagined for himself, but he loves the life he has now.

'It all came together so brilliantly,' he says. 'Gemma and I both loved dogs and now, along with the kids and one another, they're our life. We have Frankie, Gemma's English Bulldog Cookie and Chelsea, a mixed-breed dog we rescued from Spain after we went on a rescue puppy training course out there. We each had to work with a rescue puppy for five days and at the end we couldn't leave either of them behind! The other one lives with Gemma's mum.

'I feel so lucky that I met Gemma; she's gorgeous. We live and work together and life is good.'

I know Jamie feels lucky, but I believe we make our own luck in life. He found his purpose, and the woman of his dreams, because he didn't give up on himself and he kept that sense of purpose throughout his recovery. He worked incredibly hard to recover from his injuries and then he went along to the dog-training classes and made an effort to get involved.

It only confirms for me that often we can't think our way into our life's passion and purpose, we have to do something to find our way in.

Setting Goals

I constantly set myself goals. When I was first in recovery, my goal was simply to get up and walk. Now my goal might be to raise money for my Foundation, or to write my next book. Either way, a goal can feel immense, but when broken down into small steps, pursuing it can feel more manageable and reachable. Each time you tick off one of your smaller goals you can see proof that you have achieved something, and that sense of achievement helps to nurture and grow your confidence. That's why goals are so important. They give us both motivation and vision. We have something to do now, and something to work towards.

How to Set Goals

You can set goals for any area of your life, but it's important to make sure they're always positive – I will do something, rather than decide that I won't. 'I won't eat chocolate' is a lot less likely to work than 'I will eat healthy foods'. Then you need to get as specific as possible: 'I will eat green vegetables twice a day, every day', for instance.

In my book *Things Get Better* I explained the SMART acronym for setting goals, which has become a popular tool in all kinds of management and lifestyle fields. I still use it to set my own goals because it's so effective and easy to remember.

SMART stands for:

 S – Specific
 M – Measurable
 A – Achievable
 R – Relevant
 T – Time-bound

What it means is this:

Choose a specific goal and then make sure it's something you can actually measure your progress towards. Ensure that the goal is achievable and that it's relevant to your life. Then set a time frame for achieving it.

For instance, you might enjoy running and decide your goal is to run a marathon. Is this something you would enjoy and that you could actually manage? (Achievable). And do you *want* to run, and do you like running (Relevant)? If so, choose which marathon to run and when (Time-bound). So you might choose the London Marathon a year from now (Specific). Then work out measurable progress – for instance, run five miles by the end of two months, ten miles after four months and so on (Measurable).

Let's take a less demanding example. Suppose you want to learn to cook curry (Specific). You love cooking, you've always wanted to try making curry (Relevant) and you have the equipment and desire to give it a go (Achievable). You decide to do it this Saturday (Time-bound) and to get going you find a recipe you like, buy the ingredients and clear a couple of hours in which to do it (Measurable). Even with something reasonably straightforward like this, the SMART framework helps, because it reminds you to put aside enough time and, most importantly, to set a time limit. So many plans go awry because we think we'll do them 'sometime' or we just don't get around to making them happen. SMART helps you make it happen and gives you a sense of purpose in achieving your goal.

Purpose Matters

Having purpose in life matters, because it is what gives our lives meaning. When we have goals and we act constructively to achieve them, then we have purpose and our lives are all the richer for it. Achieving goals makes you feel good about yourself, and acting with purpose brings confidence.

Each one of us could choose to live our lives with negativity. I could have chosen to be bitter and angry, but that would have made me, and everyone around me, miserable – and what would be the point of that? You'll have your own version of this: old hurts, injustices and broken dreams that you could choose to focus on.

But how much better to focus on your abilities and strengths, your hopes and plans?

By acting with purpose you give yourself both present and future benefit. You win now because your life is meaningful, and you win in the future because you will achieve your goals. And along the way you will live a happier, fuller and more confident life.

Kindness

I think that kindness is one of the most important of all human qualities. Small acts of kindness, the sort we come across every day, are what make the world a better place. It's extraordinary how vividly we remember times when someone has been generous towards us, and the warmth we feel when thinking about it. People tell stories of kindnesses they received many years ago, and they often still speak so highly of the person who showed them that kindness.

Sometimes I think we spend an awful lot of time focused on ourselves, trying to get things right, fixating over how we can improve our looks, or career, or relationships. But perhaps the answer isn't always to try harder; maybe it's simply to do something different, to stop thinking about ourselves and to start thinking about someone else.

Studies show that when you do things for others, it makes you feel good. To be kind to someone else will enrich your own life.

Generosity of spirit – giving your time and energy, whatever the circumstances – reaps wonderful rewards. You feel better, as does the other person. It's a win-win situation. And when you are kinder to others, they are more likely to respond with warmth, which in turn makes you feel liked and appreciated, and that helps boost your confidence.

Showing kindness is about being friendly, generous and considerate. It's helping someone in need, not for your own benefit or advantage, but for theirs.

It's said that kindness makes the world go round. Certainly the world would be a poorer place without it. There's a lovely five-minute film called *Kindness Boomerang* that's been watched online by over 23 million people. It's about how kindness gets passed on. It starts with a man helping a little boy who falls off his skateboard. The little boy then carries an elderly woman's shopping and the elderly woman helps someone in turn. The act of kindness is passed through several more people until the final one, a waitress, takes a glass of cold water to the hot, tired guy who first helped the little boy up.

The message is that what you give out can come back to you, often from an unexpected source. And the goodwill generated by a small act of kindness can send waves of warmth and generosity rippling outwards.

So it pays to be kind to others – and to be kind to yourself, too. That's harder, isn't it? But it's a habit worth cultivating, because, believe it or not, you deserve kindness just as much as the next person.

Kindness is Good for Us

A great deal of research has been done on the links between kindness and self-esteem, happiness and confidence. And all the studies indicate that being kind to others is beneficial for us: it makes us feel good about ourselves and that makes us happier and more confident.

We all know that spending money on friends can often feel better than spending it on yourself. And it's been proved, too: scientific evidence shows that giving really does improve the quality of our lives. People who donate their time or money are an amazing 42 per cent more likely to be happy than those who do not give anything. The act of giving has been linked to the release of oxytocin in the body, which is also known as the feel-good hormone because it induces feelings of warmth, euphoria and rapport with others. This warm glow, known as the 'helper's high', can last for up to two hours, because the act of giving acti-vates the area of the brain known as the reward centre. So if you want to feel good – give!

People who are generous are also nicer to be around. Think about people you know who aren't kind. People who are grumpy, selfish or interested only in themselves. Are they the type of people you want to spend time with? Almost certainly not. Are they happy, confident or pleasant? Rarely.

One recent study showed that people who live in the Scandi-navian countries have the greatest sense of happiness and wellbeing of all Europeans, while inhabitants of countries from the former Soviet bloc have the least. The rest of us are somewhere in between.

In Scandinavia, the study revealed that large percentages of the population – 70 per cent in Norway – were involved in volunteer projects of various kinds. But in the less-happy countries, volunteering was almost non-existent. For example, at the time of the study, only 7 per cent of Bulgarians were volunteers.

Now, these findings obviously don't prove beyond doubt that being kind makes you happy. And it may well be true that happy and balanced people are the ones most likely to get involved in volunteer projects. Nonetheless, the research does at least suggest that kindness and altruism – regard for others – may be associated with happiness.

Those who feel miserable and negative about their life tend to grow happier when they do something for the benefit of others. Perhaps it's because believing we are useful to others is a basic need. Humans are naturally social creatures and we need to find ways to connect with one another – and there's no better way to do this than through offering out our kindness.

Kindness in My Life

Kindness from other people has been a lifeline for me during the years since I was attacked. For a long time afterwards, I was isolated and stuck at home, entirely dependent on the support and care of my family: my parents, brother and sister.

I didn't think I'd ever have a social life again. I didn't even *want* friends at that point, because I was scared of human contact and essentially just wanted to hide. I didn't have a mobile phone or email address, so I wasn't in touch with anyone and I imagined that all my friends had moved on. Although a few had, in truth there were many who had not, and who refused to give up on me.

They came to visit, and did their best to encourage me and try to make me laugh again. I'm so grateful to them for sticking by me through the hardest times. Their kindness helped to restore my faith in human nature.

For a long time I suffered from agoraphobia, which meant I was afraid of going outside and refused to leave the house, despite my parents' encouragement. It was partly because I had no idea where I could go that wouldn't result in me being stared at, judged and criticised. The only place I could think of where I hoped people might not judge me was our local church. Eventually I found the courage to go along to a small group that met there every week. I wasn't religious, I just wanted somewhere that felt safe, and that's what I found. The people there were tolerant and non-judgemental, they welcomed me and included me, and I found a lot of comfort and hope through going to the weekly meetings. It helped me take my first step back into the world.

Mum would drive me to the church and I'd duck inside and find the welcome and acceptance that I desperately needed. I cried so many times in that church, and sometimes I got angry, too. I was full of questions – why did this happen to me? How would I get through it? Whatever I said, the others in the group listened to me without judgement. Their kindness got me through that terrible time. Years later, in November 2015, it was the pastor from that church, a kind and generous man who has known me since those early days, who married me and Richie. In his speech he said, 'We prayed for someone wonderful for Katie, and here he is!' It meant so much to me that he was involved in our wedding.

Once I started work on the Katie Piper Foundation, I began to see how many people will give help to others just because they can. All kinds of people made contributions or offered to assist us in practical ways. One of the first was Simon Cowell, who offered his help after having seen my documentary, and he's still involved with the Foundation today. Simon and many others support the Foundation just because they want to. They are in the fortunate position of being able to help and so they do; they choose to give, without expecting anything in return. It has proved to me that if you are trying to do something good, your efforts will attract good people to help you.

As the Foundation got underway, we relied heavily on volunteers who gave up their time to help us with all kinds of tasks, from answering the phones to running burns workshops. The volunteers who got involved provided me not just with support for the Foundation but with friendship. And through the workshops, I began to meet other survivors and to forge relationships and friendships with them. People were grateful I was in their lives and I was grateful they were in mine. Their company, support and friendship meant a great deal to me.

Despite my new friends, I believed, for a long time, that I would never find one special person to be with in my life, so to help fill that void I kept myself as busy as possible. I took up things like marathon training and acting classes, searching for ways to bring new people into my life, people that I could talk to, share experiences with and look forward to spending time with. I began to put myself out there and what came back in return was an extraordinary amount of kindness.

Because of what happened to me, I've been put in a position where I get to see just how much people care. Of course there are some who are cruel and unkind, but there are far more who are wonderfully kind and who go out of their way to offer help, love, support, encouragement and laughter.

When I met Richie, in 2012, I discovered the kindest man I've ever known. His humour, generosity and warmth had a profound influence on me. In the years that we've been together he has never once shouted at me, never been unkind. It's in his nature to see the good side of everything and, for reasons I still puzzle over, he fell in love with me.

Richie and I get on so well because we are kind to each other. That's what our relationship is built on. Being kind to him and kind to my daughter Belle makes me happy. I love kindness! It's what makes life worthwhile.

The Kindness of Others

It's easy to underestimate the importance of kindness in our lives. Few of our accomplishments and achievements, whatever those are, can be managed alone. In many ways we are the sum of other people's kindness, whether they are our family, colleagues, friends or strangers. And kindness can make a huge difference to our confidence, because when people are kind to us we feel worthwhile.

It's great to think about all those people who have helped you on your way, whose kind actions or words have set you on a path or ensured that something worked out for you, and who gave you a hand when you needed it.

A lot of these people won't even know that they made a difference. Someone may have brightened your day with a small act of kindness, like giving you a lift or buying you lunch, and this may have raised your mood such that later in the day you were able

145

to do something a little bit better, go the extra mile, finish a piece of work or achieve something you'd hoped for.

Unexpected acts of kindness always amaze me. When you are shown kindness by individuals who are not your family and friends, whether it is a gesture of time, advice or affection, it's a wonderful surprise. Unexpected kindnesses affirm that you are worth something, that people care about you for no other reason than simply wanting to. When that happens (and if you watch out for it, you'll see that in fact it happens all the time), it gives you a glow, boosts your self-esteem, makes you smile and encourages you to do the same for other people.

A few years back, a very successful couple got in touch with the Foundation to offer us help. The husband runs businesses in China, Asia, Britain and America, and he is phenomenally busy – the type of person who starts his day at 6am and doesn't finish until 9pm. And yet he found the time to become a patron of the Foundation, and to encourage his contacts in the corporate world to come along to events like our annual fundraising ball, to buy tables and place bids in the auction. His wife is a make-up artist and she had seen my first documentary, *My Beautiful Face*. She now helps us run make-up workshops for survivors. This couple donate their time to the Foundation and to me, and I know that I can call them at any time for advice or help and they will be there. They have never asked me for anything in return.

These two kind people continue to make a difference to my life and to the lives of survivors every day. They, along with many others who have touched my life, have proved to me that there are decent and good people all around us. Kindness is a force for good and it has the power to offset some of the bad things that happen in the world. It's because of people's kindness that I am a more confident person and I choose to see the world as a good place.

The Value of Friends

Finding a relationship that makes you happy is a wonderful thing. But it's not everything. Friends – people who love and care for you, and who understand you – are so important, too. Real friends are the ones who are there for life, through all the ups and downs of dating, relationships and break-ups, career changes, arguments, losses and challenges. It's your friends who provide a shoulder when you need it, not to mention laughter, companionship and kindness. Good friends are like diamonds: they're rare and precious and when you have one, you really value them.

Most of us have friends we've made at different stages of life – school, college, work, those we've met playing sports or attending clubs, or fellow parents. Out of all of these people, there are only ever a handful that become really close friends, the kind you can talk to about anything, call in the middle of the night or rely on in a crisis.

So while it's fine, and certainly fun, to have hundreds of Facebook 'friends' and a good many acquaintances, your real friends are the ones you know you can turn to, and who will readily turn to you, over and over again.

It isn't just experience that tells me how important friends are. The evidence for the power of friendship is overwhelming. It's been proved that having a support network is crucial if we are to be happy and healthy – both physically and mentally – and indeed to live longer.

For a friendship to work, it needs to be two-way. We've all had relationships with someone who insists they're our friend but whose company in reality just leaves us feeling drained.

A real friend is someone you like and are always pleased to see, who you find stimulating and uplifting, and who gives you as much as you give them. A real friend helps to build your confidence, through believing in you and encouraging you.

But to have a friend, you first need to *be* a friend – and that means being willing to go the extra mile for someone else, offering kindness and support when they need it and taking a genuine interest in who they are and the life they lead.

Making Friends

Not everyone finds it easy to make friends. But even if you are shy or unsure of yourself, you can still be open to making new friends. It just takes a bit of effort.

Think about adults you know – friends and colleagues and relatives. Are there some you prefer to be with? People who radiate positive energy and leave you with a sense of optimism and motivation when you part? Those sorts of individuals are usually happy and contented. And we are attracted to them, like moths to a flame. They are good to be around and we look forward to seeing them. When you find a person you feel drawn to, whose company you enjoy, don't be afraid to pursue the possibility of friendship, perhaps by asking them if they want to go for a coffee, or inviting them for lunch. It may or may not grow into a strong friendship, but if you don't get to know them, you'll never find out.

If you're not meeting new people through your job and usual

activities, then go out of your way to find potential friends by going to places where others will be – you could join a sports club, volunteer locally, or find an activity you'd like to take part in. Make the effort to start talking to other people, and sooner or later you are bound to find someone you click with. Remember that everyone out there is a potential friend you just haven't met yet. And remember to smile!

Kindness to Yourself

You can't give much to others if you don't look after yourself first. Kindness starts at home – with you.

Being kind to yourself begins with basic self-care, such as eating well, exercising and getting enough sleep. It's amazing how many people neglect to look after themselves and then wonder why they get ill or feel tired all the time. We all know that sleep deprivation, bad food and lack of exercise leaves us feeling irritable and snappy, with a brain like fog.

I have to look after myself, because managing everything that I squeeze into my life requires a lot of energy. I also have ongoing healthcare needs – doctors and operations will always be a part of my life – so I need to make sure that I give myself the best possible chance of a quick recovery each time. I've learned to feed myself healthily, ensure I get enough rest and exercise in ways I enjoy, all of which support my body in doing everything that it does for me. I want to set a good example for Belle, too, by showing her that self-care isn't a luxury, it's a necessity. Beyond the basics, I like to spoil myself every now and then, with an evening at home, candles, a great film to watch and a chance to just relax.

Self-care is all about balance, so we need to allow ourselves these quiet, nurturing times after the chaos of running around all day. We need time alone as well as time with our family and friends.

Kindness and Self-Esteem

Back in Chapter 2 I talked about self-esteem: that feeling inside that tells us we're basically OK, no matter what happens on the outside. And here it is again, because to be a kind person you need to see yourself as essentially good and worthwhile. If you don't think much of yourself and don't treat yourself with kindness, you are less likely to extend kindness to others.

Human beings have the most amazing capacity for kindness, love, decency and goodness. But when people have poor self-esteem, they can find it difficult to recognise these important qualities in themselves. We all have goodness inside us, but sometimes we just can't see it and instead choose to see ourselves as cold, unfeeling, hard or distant. As a result, we lose touch with the warm, caring, personable part of our nature.

I recently met Sally, who told me her story. A couple of years back, Sally was made redundant. It was no reflection on her abilities – the company was in financial trouble and was making hundreds of people redundant. But somehow Sally saw the redundancy as confirmation that she was ineffective and stupid.

Feeling terribly low and unsure about the way forward, she decided to go to a therapist. She had a whole laundry list of things that she believed were wrong with her, and when the therapist asked her to think of good things about herself she was lost for words.

'I honestly thought there was nothing,' Sally told me. 'But the therapist insisted that I must have done one good thing in my life, and so eventually – after a lot of thought – I told him that I had helped my neighbour when she broke her leg. The neighbour lived alone, so I used to go and get her shopping for her, and go in for a chat. I enjoyed it; at the time I didn't really think of it as kindness or doing good. But when I told the therapist about it I suddenly felt very tearful. I remembered how grateful my neighbour was and how she said she looked forward to my visits. We became good friends and we still see each other now.

'It took that therapist to remind me that I can be a good and kind person.'

When I asked Sally why she had found it so hard to see her own good qualities, she thought for a minute.

'I think it's because my mum was always very tough on me. She had a "not good enough" attitude to everything I did and I used to feel I got everything wrong when I was around her.'

It was Sally's low self-esteem, a legacy of her childhood, that stopped her seeing her own goodness, her value and her worth. And the redundancy just exacerbated it. But after learning to take a more balanced view of herself, Sally stopped putting herself down and started looking for a new job. She soon found a job she enjoyed more than the old one, and these days she's very happy. 'I'm good at my job,' she told me, laughing. 'And I'm a kind person, I really enjoy doing things for other people.'

Keep a 'Goodness' Record

Do you recognise your own goodness? If the answer is no, then it's worth starting a Goodness Record. Every day, write down three good and kind things that you have done – it might be putting a coin in a busker's hat, sharing your newspaper, buying a colleague a coffee, giving up your seat to someone who needed it more, or texting a friend who needed cheering up.

Think back and remember some of the good things you did in the past, too – as a child or as a younger adult.

This daily 'Goodness Record' may seem like blowing your own trumpet, but the truth is we all need to do that now and then. It will help you to become aware of the goodness and kindness that you generate.

You might also start writing down when someone has been kind to you. Because that will remind you that others are kind to you because you matter, because you're worth it and you deserve it.

When you're kind to someone else, or someone is kind to you, it creates a bond between the two of you. And that bond – the kindness bond – is a powerful connection. That's why kindness is so important: it can unite us in a way that nothing else can.

Being in touch with goodness – our own and other people's – feeds our souls and helps us believe that:

- We are valuable to ourselves and other people.
- Life is worth living.
- We have rights.
- We are deserving of love.

Try it and see!

The Power of Kindness

I heard this story recently, and like so many of the great stories about kindness, it stuck in my mind for days, as a wonderful reminder of the effect that acts of kindness can have.

A policeman in a small town in the north of England popped into a supermarket for some groceries and noticed that the teenager who helped him had wound duct tape around his worn-down shoe.

It was raining outside as the teenager helped the policeman to put the groceries into his car.

'What's with the duct tape?' he asked the boy. 'Is that some kind of fashion statement I don't know about?'

The boy looked embarrassed. 'No, it's just that my shoe split and I can't afford new ones until pay day.'

'And how long is it until pay day?' the policeman asked.

'Two weeks,' the boy replied.

The following day the policeman went and bought a new pair of shoes and took them to the shop, where he found the boy and gave them to him.

The boy was stunned. 'I'll pay you back on pay day,' he said. But the policeman grinned and said, 'Don't worry, just pay it forward.'

Paying it forward – passing on a gesture of kindness, which doesn't have to be as expensive as buying a pair of shoes, it can just be a simple, considerate act to another person is a great concept. Hopefully the boy will have done something equally kind for someone else, and they for the next person, and so on, thereby passing kindness around the world.

Ways to be Kind

You will nearly always be rewarded personally for any act of kindness. The more that you choose to give out to people, the more joy, gratitude and appreciation you will receive, which can all add to your sense of confidence in life. Whenever you're feeling down, challenged, stressed or low in confidence, it can pay to do something kind for someone else as you'll indirectly be doing yourself a big personal favour. So find ways to be kind every day, to yourself and to others. As with the paying it forward idea, it needn't involve money, it can be any generous or helpful gesture. That could mean listening to someone who needs to talk, or lending them a hand. Keep it simple: you don't have to solve everyone's problems, just look for small ways to make the world a slightly better place and other people's lives a tiny bit better. Do something to make them smile, even if it's just making them a cup of tea.

Kindness is infectious, so don't hesitate to pass it along!

CHAPTER 10

Bouncing Back

Life's an exciting journey, but it's also unpredictable. Good things happen, sometimes wonderful things, but bad things happen, too – to all of us. There are no guarantees about what is ahead. The key lies in how we cope with those things, both the good and the bad. When we can take anything in our stride, knowing that we'll cope whatever comes along, then we have developed resilience – that inner strength of spirit that says 'I'll get through this and bounce back, no matter what'.

Family stresses, work problems, ill health and the loss of those you love – few people avoid at least some of these things happening in their lives. So when you are knocked down by life, how do you find that ability to come back stronger than ever? How do you learn to see failure as just another step along the road, and to rise anew from the ashes of heartache or loss? How do you cope with a sudden drastic change in your life and still carry on undeterred?

The answer to all these questions is resilience, that bounce-back ability that some people just seem to have naturally. But the good news is that if you don't already have a generous share of this excellent quality, there are ways you can develop it in yourself.

Resilience is a great quality to have. It stops you from feeling hopeless when life throws tough problems your way. Resilience allows us to adapt, to see the bright side, to look ahead and find a way through. And resilience is strongly correlated with confidence; highly resilient people also have high confidence levels. That's not surprising, because the two are closely linked; if you can face difficulties and trust you will bounce back, you will have the confidence to cope with whatever difficulties you encounter.

I had to discover my own resilience at a time when the choice seemed to be between letting myself go under or finding a way to survive. After the attack, when I came round from the coma in hospital and realised what had happened to me, terrible as it was, I remember that there was some part of me, deep inside, that wanted so badly to live. I was young, I hadn't lived my life yet and I wasn't ready to have it snuffed out. I didn't know what kind of life I was facing, but I knew that – whatever it was – I wanted it. I wanted to be here and to survive. So that was my starting point, and I think it was that little seed of resilience that got me through everything else. I just wasn't ready to give in. I was stubborn, I was determined and I was angry – why should someone else get to take my life away from me?

Every day I thought, well, at least I'm a little bit better than yesterday. And that kept me going, moving gradually forward, even if it was in very small increments, perhaps just the ability to manage an exercise a little better, or spending the day in a little less pain.

I had a lot of people on my side, and that really helped. Not just my family and friends but also the extraordinary hospital staff who worked so hard on my behalf. They all gave me so much support, and one of the other things that kept me going was the feeling that I couldn't bear to let them down.

Most important of all, though, was the part of me that thought: this is something horrible that's happened to me, but it isn't everything. I'm not going to let it wipe out the rest of my life; one day it's going to be just one memory, just one part of my life that's now behind me and there will be so much more ahead.

Whatever difficulties you have faced, or are facing now, remember your inner resilience. Find it, and use it. In this chapter I will share some great tips and exercises to help you harness that inner strength and learn to tell yourself, 'This is not all there is, I will get through it and there will be better times waiting.'

The Science of Resilience

Resilience is so important that some psychologists call it the ultimate art of living. It can make a huge difference to your life, and in a crisis situation it can even be what keeps you alive.

Scientific studies of super-resilient people – those who have survived disasters and major traumas – show that they believe in themselves and, most important of all, they believe in the future.

To put it in a nutshell, resilient people see a bad event as temporary, rather than letting it become everything. It's not that they suffer any less, but they know that there is something beyond their immediate troubles. In this way, resilient people refuse to let hardship or misfortune define them.

Imagine you lost all your money and had to declare yourself

bankrupt. A less-resilient person might see themselves as incapable and a failure, and that might limit their choices in life after the bankruptcy. A resilient person, on the other hand, might see it as a temporary setback, something to learn from and a jumping-off point for a fresh start and, ultimately, better things.

Scientists say that differences in resilience seem to be genetic – some people are just born more resilient. But resilience can also be cultivated. We can strengthen self-belief and our sense of being able to cope; we can build up our mental flexibility and become more resilient over time.

Looking at what we've done in the past is the first step. We all have strengths; we have all coped with difficult situations. And the coping mechanisms we developed at the time are still there. So when thinking about traumas we have been through, rather than looking at the events themselves, we need to turn our attention to how we *coped* with them, so that we become aware of our strengths, instead of what we might imagine is our weakness. Every time we overcome adversity – whether that is violence, emotional pain or loss, we become stronger. That's why there are people who have been through unimaginable ordeals and yet are strong and effective in their present lives, without bitterness or self-pity.

When we continue to view ourselves as victims, we don't feel any need to change. We attract sympathy, we put our efforts into trying to make people understand how much we have suffered and as a result we find ourselves stuck. But when you decide not to be a victim any longer, that's when you find your inner strength.

Those people who don't buy into the idea that a troubled childhood leads to a troubled adult life, often manage to turn their lives around and become successful. Instead of their childhood hardships being like a ball and chain, holding them back, they bounce back and emerge as strong, resilient adults.

Sometimes hardship in childhood – for instance living with alcoholic, violent or neglectful parents – makes children determined not to repeat the pattern and they become stronger and make much better choices. They maintain their self-esteem despite the influence of their parents.

Resilient people also remember what they've done well – they appreciate their own successes and take responsibility for them. And they take charge of their problems, looking for solutions, while at the same time turning to others around them, people they trust, for support and help.

The Resilience Exercise

Here's a nice little exercise that really helps to illustrate what resilience is all about.

Stand up with your shoulders stooped and your head bowed, as if you're acting the part of someone very tired, down and defeated. In this position what can you see? Nothing beyond the ground and your own feet. Your range of vision is very limited indeed.

Now raise your head and push back your shoulders, very slowly. Notice how, as your head comes up, you can see further ahead, and once you are upright, you can see towards the horizon. Now your field of vision is huge, you can see all kinds of things that you couldn't see when your head was down.

These two positions represent the person who lacks resilience and the one who has it. With resilience you can see all the possibilities ahead, even if at this moment life is very hard.

So be the resilient person: keep your shoulders back and your head up and look at all the possibilities there are ahead of you.

Optimism

We all know that some people are more optimistic than others, people who are more hopeful about the future than others. In fact, it's not uncommon for the parents of three children who were all born within a few years to feel bewildered as to why one is a 'ray of sunshine', one is moody and yet another is very quiet but confident. How can three children who have the same parents and who all live in the same house be so different? It's something that the nature versus nurture debaters are still trying to work out.

What is known is that there are definite links between optimism and resilience. Optimistic people tend to be more resilient than pessimistic people because they seem to have more get-up-and-go, and enjoy life more. On the other hand, there are many individuals who are quiet and reflective and not obviously optimistic who are good at getting through tough times and not giving up. So I guess the answer is that you don't have to be an optimistic person to be resilient, but it probably helps!

I think I was an optimist before the attack, so I had that on my side. But as I recovered I had to dig deep for the inner resources to keep me going and to rediscover my optimism. I found a few books and tapes that helped me a lot; I used to listen to an audiobook version of *The Secret*, by Rhonda Byrne, during the four, hour-long, daily sessions of massage and exercises that my parents had to do with me. I'd been given it by a friend and at first I thought it wasn't my kind of thing, but as I listened to it it really did help me to focus my mind on success and possibilities, rather than my failures, my difficulties and my pain.

Use Past Strengths

We can all become more resilient by identifying the strengths that we've developed through the years – and then working out how we can harness these strengths to assist us in solving current or future problems.

Looking back into the past, we can all remember difficult times that we survived, however big or small. Most of us have come through the break-up of a friendship, family rows, the end of a relationship, the loss of a loved pet or an upheaval at home or work. So when we feel overwhelmed by life's challenges, it can help if we remind ourselves that we've already got experience in dealing with problems, and encourage ourselves to remember what the skills were that we used before.

For example, I know a woman, Lisa, who has been going through prolonged treatment for cancer. It's been really difficult and she says it's the toughest thing she's ever had to deal with. But she told me recently how she has managed to get through it. Fifteen years ago, as a single mum with a toddler and few prospects, she studied for a degree. That had been tough, too. Very. But she had done it by surrounding herself with supportive friends, planning her schedule so she could get enough work done while looking after her daughter and giving herself little treats and rewards when she was feeling low.

During the cancer treatment she realised that there were parallels between the two situations and it occurred to her that she could use the strategies she had evolved 15 years earlier to get her through her illness.

So, she kept in touch with good friends and made sure she spoke to them or saw them as much as possible. She planned her schedule so that she would have quiet days when she knew she'd be feeling rough after the chemo, but would devise trips to the cinema or dinner with her daughter or a visit to her sister on her 'good' days. She also built in treats for herself to pick her up on treatment days – like a new book to read when she got home.

She said to me, 'When I was first diagnosed I didn't think I had the strength to deal with my illness. But by remembering how I got through my degree, I helped myself to be stronger and more resilient.'

I guess we can all learn something from Lisa's story, which is that in tough times we can become more resilient by looking at our strengths and our past triumphs and using all these things to help our minds to focus on what we can do rather than what we can't.

What's Stopping You?

When you are facing some difficulty that seems insurmountable, write down a list of the thoughts that are stopping you from dealing with it.

They are likely to be something like this:

- This is too hard.
- I'm bound to fail.
- Maybe I should try to forget about it for now.
- It's too much for me.
- What's the point anyway?

When you have your list, look at each point in turn and see if you can find an alternative thought to replace it.

Something like this:

- This is very hard, but I need to remember that I have come through tough times before and therefore I can do so again. I will try to recall what made me strong before and do my best to use the same tactics that worked back then.
- I do fear failure, but I am not the sort of person who gives up easily, and today I am going to think of two things that might help me to start dealing with this problem. Perhaps if I can take it a step at a time, I will gradually find a way of dealing with it.
- I could try to forget about all this now, but actually even if I go out with friends or have a few drinks I'm pretty sure the problem will be at the back of my mind. So, perhaps I should face up to it and start trying to sort it. I'll talk to a friend who's had some bad times and see if he/she has any advice to offer.
- It feels too much, but I'm stronger than I realise and I can do this. What do I need to do to help me feel stronger? Perhaps remembering past times that I've been strong enough to get through will help.
- If I let hopelessness take over I'll never get past this. And I want to. I want to move past it to better things in the future. So I'm going to start working on it right now.

Once you get your mind into problem-solving mode, you'll be amazed at how much you can achieve.

The Glass Half-full

One of the biggest shifts that resilient people make is from the glass half-empty to the glass half-full.

Which are you? A glass-half-empty person or a glass-half-full one?

Here's one of the ways in which psychologists help us to make the shift from one to the other.

> *Think about a difficult time in your childhood or teenage years. Perhaps you were in trouble at school, or with your parents. Perhaps you did something you shouldn't have done. Or it may be that you were blamed for something you didn't do and punished unfairly.*
>
> *Re-tell the story of what happened, with you as the hero. Maybe you were clever and got out of trouble. Or maybe you took the punishment bravely. Maybe you learned how to do things differently, or made an important decision.*

The way you choose to interpret events is so powerful. So why not choose to interpret them in a way that recognises your strengths and allows you to move forward feeling good about yourself?

A World of Possibilities – Joe's Story

Joe was someone I met through a friend a couple of years ago and I could see straight away that he was a glass-half-empty guy. At 31 he was good-looking, clever and he had a lot going for him, but he just couldn't see it. He had a safe job working in a bank, but he found it boring and he dreamed of finding something else – except he knew he didn't have the courage to leave what seemed like such a secure position.

Then Joe's father became gravely ill. His mother had died when he was a teenager and Joe and his father had always been close, so when he learned that his father had only a few months to live, Joe took the decision to give up his job and spend the time with his father.

They had four and a half months together, and Joe was with his father to the end. But after his father's death, Joe felt his life was at a complete standstill. He had no job, no close relatives, few friends and no idea what to do with himself. He was grieving and he felt lost.

One day, about two months after his father's death, Joe bumped into Sarah, a girl he'd worked with at the bank. He had always liked her, so when she invited him for a coffee he said yes, and as they sat in the cafe over their lattes she asked him about his plans.

'I don't really have any,' Joe told her. 'All I can see is endings. I guess I'll have to apply for a job in another bank, but for some reason I keep putting it off.'

'I'm not surprised,' Sarah said. 'I got the impression you didn't like the bank job much. I didn't either; I'm back at college now, doing an art course. Isn't there something else you'd rather do?'

Joe was surprised; he hadn't even considered that he might do something else. He thought for a bit. 'Well, I did always want to travel, but I could never find the time or the money.'

'Why not do it now then?' Sarah asked. 'You're free, there's nothing stopping you, you're still young and you could go to all the places you've dreamed of.'

'What about finding a job?' Joe said. 'I ought to be doing that.'

'Do it when you get back,' Sarah smiled. 'You might have a few new ideas by then.'

After he'd said goodbye to Sarah, and promised to call her for another coffee again soon, Joe couldn't stop thinking about the idea of travelling. His father had left him a little money, and he realised that there was nothing stopping him – apart from the limitations he set on himself.

It took Joe a few more weeks to begin the shift from glass-half-empty to glass-half-full, but bit by bit he became more excited, as he planned to spend a year travelling around the world. He called Sarah to tell her and, as she shared his delight, he suggested she come and join him for a couple of weeks when he got to Italy, so that she could study the art. Sarah said she'd love to.

Eighteen months later Joe was back and busy with his new career as a photographer. He'd taken a camera with him around the world and had fallen in love with photography. He also had a new girlfriend – Sarah had joined him in Italy and again in Kenya and they had fallen in love.

Joe could have taken the safe route, the glass-half-empty route, into another dull job and a predictable life. Instead he chose to change, and when he lifted his eyes to the horizon he found all kinds of possibilities waiting for him. He took the glass-half-full route and let himself trust that everything would work out. And it did.

The Steps to Resilience

Here are ten steps you can take that will help you develop inner strength, resilience and bounce-back ability!

Don't wait for problems to disappear

In other words, when you have a problem, do something. Taking action helps you to feel in charge and reminds you that you're not helpless; you can make changes, even if you can't instantly solve everything. Focusing on making changes will make you feel a lot better than doing nothing. Start by making a quick list of ideas, things that you think may help the situation.

Remind yourself of your strengths and accomplishments

A bit of positive self-talk can go a long way when you're under stress. So take a moment to think about all that you've done and all that you are – strong, determined, wise and capable.

Turn to your friends

At a time of stress or crisis, we need our friends. So it's important that we nurture and cherish friendships – and family relationships, too. Having someone to talk to at a difficult time won't make the problem go away, but it will give you comfort, support and someone else's outlook on the problem.

Be flexible

The more flexible and adaptable you are, the better you will cope with challenging times. If you're very rigid about the way you do things and lead your life, you'll find it harder to cope. Flexibility means you'll be more able to take change of any kind in your stride and thrive in new situations. And it means you're more likely to keep looking for solutions until you find one.

Look after yourself

You'll cope better with a crisis if you get enough sleep, eat well and exercise regularly. Looking after your own needs and staying healthy will make you better able to face the tough stuff when it comes along.

Remember to think of the future

You can't stop stressful things happening, but you can remember that, however tough the present moment is, things may feel very different in the future. Imagine you've been made redundant. It can be terrifying, but if you visualise you in a year's time in a job you like even better it really will help you with the challenges you face right now.

Accept change

Things are always going to change. Both the good and the bad in life eventually pass, and new things come along. So don't fight it – change can feel hard, but it's normal and not a terrible thing. A new home feels strange until it becomes familiar, and then it's not a new home any more, it's just home.

Keep busy

In a crisis, doing something is better than doing nothing. Not only because that way things get done, but because when your hands are busy, your mind becomes more ordered and calm. Sounds strange, but it's a proven fact. So if nothing else, put the kettle on.

Do it now!

Deal with issues and challenges as they come along – don't be the type of person who puts things off and hopes they'll go away. If you're used to paying a bill when it arrives, or making that difficult call now and not in three days' time, then you'll be ready to cope much better with a crisis.

Be an optimist

I know, this one isn't easy if it doesn't come naturally to you. But it's worth working at looking on the glass-half-full, bright side of life, because it really will help you in difficult times. Pick a few simple affirmations – life is good, things always work out in the end, I can cope with anything – and use them every day.

Out of the Blue – Jessie's Story

Jessie MacDonald was a pretty teenager of 17 with a great life. She had a loving family – including five brothers and sisters – a nice home and two dogs and two horses she loved. At school she had loads of friends and she was looking forward to going to university to study to become a primary school teacher.

Then she developed a pain in her right leg. Eventually it got bad enough that her mum took her to the doctor, who referred her to a specialist. He diagnosed a Giant Cell Tumour (GCT) in her leg. Doctors warned her that she might lose her leg, or even die, because the tumour could develop secondary tumours in her lungs.

Overnight Jessie's world changed. Nothing was certain any longer.

'I was stunned,' Jessie says. 'It was shocking. But I kept believing that everything would be all right.'

Doctors operated within days of the diagnosis, in March 2013, and they managed to remove the entire tumour from Jessie's femur – the bone that goes from hip to knee. It was great news, and apart from a long scar, Jessie's leg was intact. But with weeks of physiotherapy in front of her, she had to drop out of her A-level year.

A few months later, in September, Jessie re-started her A levels. Then the tumour returned. Once again, her life was turned upside down. In November she had her second operation in a year and the new tumour was removed.

'They hoped they had got it all, and this time I didn't drop out of A levels because I didn't want to get any further behind,' Jessie says. 'So I studied as I recovered. I had two long scars down my leg, but apart from that I was fine.'

Despite all the obstacles that were standing in her way, Jessie went on to pass her A levels and get into Roehampton University, where she started studying to become a teacher in the autumn of 2015. She also found time to raise funds for the hospital where she had been treated, the Royal National Orthopaedic Hospital in Stanmore, London.

In the spring of 2015 Jessie was the youngest participant in our Ideal Home Show Diversity Catwalk. She looked amazing and her confidence just shone through. So what got Jessie through such a tough experience at such a young age?

'I have a fantastic family and great friends,' Jessie says. 'They all helped me and gave me so much love and support.

'I think something like what happened to me could either leave you really depressed and down or be the making of you. For me, that's what it was. I was so glad to come through it, so grateful to the doctors and nursing staff and I felt I had my life back. I wanted to make the most of it.

'I've got scars and I'll always have them, but they're part of me now, this is who I am.

'I've always been pretty confident, so I'm sure that helped. But I had always taken everything I had for granted. Going through cancer, and almost losing it all, made me appreciate everything so much more. It also taught me to appreciate other people's situations. I met so many people worse off that I was.

'The diversity catwalk was the same. The women I met there were inspirational, powerful and amazing. They had all been through such tough times, and they had all come out stronger than ever.

'What I learned was that no matter what life throws at you, there's always a light at the end of the tunnel. It's fine to feel sorry for yourself, but then you have to get back up again and realise that you will get through it.'

People like Jessie make me want to cheer. She was so young when she became ill, and yet she coped so beautifully. Jessie had all the elements of resilience in place and she was able to come through a very scary situation, two operations, weeks of recovery and a second start to her A levels and still keep a positive outlook.

What Jessie proved was that nothing need break your spirit. There's a saying I love – 'Life isn't about waiting for the storms to pass, it's about learning to dance in the rain.' Don't hide away when tough times come along, go out and face them and find the blessings in them.

Don't let anything break you; keep your spirit intact. Be your own superhero. And never, ever let go of hope.

CHAPTER
11

Peace of Mind

I've always been a bit of a worrier. In fact, I can worry about anything – what to have for dinner, what to wear tomorrow, whether my train will be on time. So you can imagine that when it comes to the big events I go into worry overdrive. When I was planning my wedding I worried about every little detail, driving Richie mad in the process.

I'm the kind of person who spends a lot of time thinking 'what if . . . ?'. I imagine dreadful scenarios and I can keep myself awake thinking about everything that could go wrong the next day.

Not surprisingly, I find it really hard to relax, let life unfold and trust that all will be well. Even the evidence that most of the time things work out fine isn't enough to stop me worrying that next time it might just all go wrong.

I've had to try hard to be less anxious and to let life unfold, and luckily I've had some great people around to help me with it. Richie is brilliant, he's not a worrier and he has taught me a lot about looking on the bright side and, when little things do go wrong, laughing instead of getting all worked up about it. And then there's my friend Kamran Bedi. Kamran was one of my flatmates in London before the attack, and he was one of the first on the scene afterwards. He ran to help me and stayed by my side as I waited for an ambulance.

Kamran has been a fantastic friend to me, sticking by me all the way through the tough months and years of treatments and recovery. He's one of those people whose company is great and who makes you feel better just by being around.

When we were flatmates Kamran was a professional dancer. He worked on shows like *The X Factor* and *Britain's Got Talent* and he danced at private functions for celebrities like Lady Gaga and Cheryl Fernandez-Versini. In between jobs he trained as a Pilates teacher and I remember him telling me how he had found so much more purpose and meaning working with individuals on a personal level. Most of his clients had injuries that he was helping them to recover from and he was so happy about helping them to do that. And, perhaps inevitably, he began to feel his life should go in a different direction.

Over the next few years Kamran added breathing and meditation to his teaching so that he could help his clients find a sense of calm and relaxation. When I set up the Foundation I invited him to host a well-being workshop, where he taught Pilates sessions, breathing techniques and short, guided meditations for relaxation.

Kamran went on to train as a life coach and hypnotherapist and to work with people on rehabilitating their bodies and their lives. He teaches his clients, and me, so much about developing a positive mental attitude and about achieving calm, peace and freedom from worry. So in this chapter I'm going to pass on some of his tips – because I think we can all benefit from feeling less worried.

Peace of Mind

It's what we'd all like a bit more of, isn't it? Peace of mind is the way we feel when we are calm and at ease, with no worries, fears or stress to trouble us. We feel happy and relaxed.

It sounds so good – and I bet you're thinking 'I never feel like that'. But actually, we all do, at times.

Think about watching a TV programme you really enjoy, or reading a great book, or lying on a beach in the sun, or being with someone whose company you love. There are times when we all experience peace of mind, we forget our troubles and worries and we're completely absorbed in what we're doing. It happens for me when I'm playing with Belle or curled up with Richie in front of a good film.

It's such a good feeling, and what we'd all like is a bit more of it. In fact, I'd like to be able to turn it on like a switch. But what gets in the way, more than anything else in life, is worry and anxiety.

The Trouble with Anxiety

Someone said to me recently, 'Worry is a total waste of time, all it does is steal your joy and keep you very busy doing nothing. 'I had to laugh, it's so true! And yet we go on worrying.

As a society we're worriers. Statistics show that one in five people feel anxious most or all of the time, and half of all of us worry more than we used to. Stress, anxiety and depression lead to 70 million lost days of work and cost the economy £70 billion to £100 billion each year.

You can be a real worrier and not even realise it, because the habit can become ingrained at a very young age. But anxiety – which is basically unease, worry and fear – takes a real toll on us. It makes us ill, spoils those times in life that we should enjoy and eats away at our physical and mental health. And when it spirals out of control, anxiety can become panic attacks, phobias and conditions like OCD – Obsessive Compulsive Disorder.

We all get anxious and worry about big events like exams, driving tests, starting a new job and so on. But some of us worry about a lot of other, everyday things. And that worry can make it hard to relax, to sleep, to eat well and to enjoy life.

There can be all kinds of causes that lead us to become anxious. Sometimes a big trauma – an accident, the loss of someone we love – can make us more anxious. Sometimes it's the result of feeling bad about ourselves as children. And sometimes it's simply that we're perfectionists and worrying becomes a way of life.

Anxiety isn't all bad news – those of us who feel anxious and worry tend to be the ones who get things done. Richie laughs at me for worrying, but it does make me a good organiser and I'm the one who stays on top of what needs to be done. But while a little bit of anxiety isn't a bad thing – and is natural – a lot can be destructive and exhausting.

There's no doubt that when we feel constantly anxious it's bad news for our confidence. High levels of anxiety often go hand-in-hand with low self-esteem and lack of confidence, which can lead us to pull back from trying new things or putting ourselves out there. To raise your confidence levels you need to reduce your anxiety.

The good news about anxiety is that there is a lot you can do to help yourself. Simple exercises and behaviours, practised regularly, can make a real difference. So now I'm going to pass on some of the wisdom and tips that Kamran has given me, and that have helped me so much:

The Traffic Jam

Anxiety is formed from the thoughts that we allow to flow through our mind. At times our minds can seem like a traffic jam of overactive thoughts about various situations, people, places, things to do, worries, concerns, fears and more. Our actions and choice of activities, along with the company we choose and the information we read or watch, can also contribute to the thoughts that we think and the anxiety that we then experience.

You may feel that the struggle to move past your anxiety is overwhelming, but you're more in control than you think and you can make things better for yourself. If you think that your situation is only going to get better with the help of an outside source then you're holding yourself back. Yes, there are various practices, coaches, classes and organisations that can help you, but you have to want to improve things and be willing to put in some effort for change to really take place. And you can make real, significant change on your own.

The reality is that dealing with anxiety is simpler than you think. It all comes down to you, your thoughts and your actions on a day-to-day basis and it starts with you becoming more self-aware.

Once you realise that you have the power to improve the way you're feeling, by changing the way that you're thinking, you can move a big step closer to overpowering any possible or present anxiety.

Start by noticing what it is that is making you anxious. This is the key to unlocking the chains of anxiety.

- Are you online a lot? Checking social media and reading about other people's lives and activities may be causing you to feel anxious about your own life.
- Are you thinking about work problems or goals?
- Are you still going over and over past events?
- Do you feel fearful about the future?
- Do you constantly find fault with the way you do things throughout the day. Is the way you talk to yourself full of 'shoulds' and 'oughts'?

Think about what's making you feel anxious. The key is not to ignore it, but to identify the cause so that you can change the effects. So just take a moment to think about the thoughts that are making you feel anxious or the activities that are leading your anxiety to build. You may want to write them down, so that you're fully aware of the root cause and you may be surprised by what comes up. Now you're not trying to ignore your anxiety or change your mind so that you forget about it. The aim is to be aware of what's building up your anxiety and then choose to relax, through your breathing, so that the anxiety no longer dominates your mind and emotions.

The Power of Breathing

The doorway through to a world of peace and relaxation is easily accessible through our breathing. This place of peace, calm and tranquillity is available in any place and at any moment that you choose. The level of peace that you can achieve is only limited by the time and effort that you put into spending time in the depths of your worrying and anxious thoughts. Your life can improve and change for the better, and you can achieve a sense of peace by taking time to slow your thoughts down.

It is through the practice of deep breathing that you can help distract your mind and also calm your emotions, as the sound of your breath can take you deep into a more calm and harmonious state where your mind can become engrossed in the simplicity of each calming breath. The benefits of deep, slow breathing go far and wide and you can experience a sense of calm and relaxation as you make the effort to think less and to breathe in a more controlled way.

When you're anxious, you tend to breathe more quickly and tense up your body. That's why relaxation is the key to you letting go and finding more peace of mind. So find somewhere comfortable to sit and start by breathing slowly. As you do, notice your breath – become aware of its sound and flow and try not to think of anything but your breathing, tuning into your breath to turn your mind away from any distracting thoughts.

Try to focus on the breath going in and out of your body so that you become distracted from over thinking and over feeling. You could even repeat the word 'calm' as you inhale and 'relax' as you exhale, over and over again in your mind to help you to achieve a sense of peace.

The more you do this, the easier it will become for you to be less distracted by your thoughts. You don't have to do it for very long. You can breathe slowly for a minute, inhaling through the nose and exhaling slowly through your mouth. See how you feel after a minute, you may want to carry on for a bit longer.

Doing this will feel like a challenge at first, but if you practise regularly it will become easier and your mind and body will feel the benefits of a simple, deep, soothing breath. It might be an idea to set a timer for five or even ten minutes and practise breathing for this length of time.

The great value of this technique is that you can do this anywhere, you don't need any equipment and nobody needs to know what you're doing.

Relaxation

While breathing exercises are at the core of relaxation, there are lots of other things you can do that will help with anxiety, stress and worry.

You could try:

- Regular exercise – it's brilliant for taking your mind off worries. Try cycling, running, walking.
- Taking a yoga class – relaxation and breathing are always part of yoga.
- Meditation classes.
- Doing more of the things that you enjoy in life – like seeing friends.
- Laughing – watch something funny or share a joke – it banishes anxiety.

Guided Relaxation

Here is a guided relaxation exercise that you can do to help yourself relax your mind as you focus on your breathing.

Find a comfortable place to sit with your back upright and your feet firmly on the ground. Close your eyes if you prefer, or choose to focus your eyes down towards your knees but keep your spine upright. Start to slowly breathe in through the nose and exhale slowly through the mouth. Let each inhale expand deep down into your abdomen, taking a full belly breath, and allow all of the air to come out of your body on each exhale. Try fifteen slow, long, deep breaths, breathing down into your belly. Allow each breath to be longer, slower and deeper and each exhale to be slower as you completely empty out your lungs. The key is to try to focus your mind on the sound and the flow of your breath. Don't worry if your mind wanders or if thoughts pop into your head, just start again by breathing in and trying to get to fifteen slow, deep, long breaths. As you focus on your breath, allow your body to relax further and further on each exhale that you take. Once you've counted fifteen slow breaths, continue to breathe at a slow, controlled rate. Don't worry about counting, just start to focus on your body. By focusing on each body part you can encourage your mind and body to connect further through the breath as you calm down and continue to distance yourself from your thoughts.

Start by focusing on your feet and feel all of the muscles of your feet and toes relaxing. Then work your way up through your body, relaxing each part bit by bit while allowing your mind to relax further as you continue to breathe slowly. Allow your calves to relax, and then all of the muscles in your legs. Slowly scan your body, moving to your pelvis area and lower back, allowing all of the muscles to relax further. Then feel your stomach relax with each breath that you take. Allow your chest to rise and fall slowly with your breath as your whole spine relaxes. As you breathe, feel your shoulders drop down and let your arms feel heavy. Now starts to focus on relaxing your jaw, your face muscles – including your forehead – and allow your eyes to feel soft. Just continue to breathe and scan your body as you encourage your mind to focus only on your breathing and your body. You may want to finish this practice by repeating the word 'relax' over and over to yourself as you sit and breathe.

It's always good to take a deep breath. The rewards are endless and also very personal to each individual. The act of consciously breathing can help you in any place and in any moment to create a sense of inner calm, and the more you practise, the easier it will become for you to feel the calming benefits that you can experience from deep breathing. Encourage yourself to invest time in creating peace in your life so that your mind can feel less anxious.

Anxiety and Confidence

Real confidence is a state of mind that you can choose or learn to develop and use for yourself in all areas of your life. Once you know how, it's easy, it's just like turning on a switch, and you can switch off anxiety and switch on confidence in an instant in any place and in any situation.

Give yourself a moment now to think back to a time where you felt completely confident. What were you doing? What comes to mind? How did you feel in that situation? What types of things were you thinking? How did you stand? Walk and talk? Allow that image of your confident memory to grow and develop in your mind and in your body as you realise that you can have that same confidence in any situation.

It all starts with your thoughts; if you're thinking negatively, or doubting yourself and allowing fear to build, that's going to influence the way that you feel and act. Try to use your mind productively and dig deep into your memory bank of confident thoughts and experiences and use the same feelings that encourage self-belief.

Confidence is a choice: it starts with our thoughts, which influence our feelings to respond in a certain way. I believe that we're only ever a single thought away from feeling confident. If we can think past any doubt or fear and change our thoughts for the better, confidence is ours for the taking.

Your Motivational Message

The critical voice that you hear inside your head can be your own worst enemy. And this inner voice can sometimes have quite a hypnotic power over you that can lead you to believe in various things that end up holding you back in life. Being self-critical can end up sounding like a broken record; however, changing the 'tune' that you have going through your head, that may be stuck on repeat, can help you to transform your life.

Try writing down a short confident paragraph or couple of lines that you can repeat to yourself in your head to silence your more critical voice. It will support you in using you mind to overpower any unconfident thoughts that are playing inside your head.

Here's an example of what you might write:

I am brave and confident, I can handle anything that comes my way, I am self-reliant and creative, I am a problem-solver, I love new situations.

The more you repeat your new motivational message, the quicker your unconscious mind will accept your new positive suggestions, leaving you to feel more confident in your mind and in your life.

Don't block your own path. The blocks that you place on yourself can only hold you back in life. So instead of feeling fearful, focus your mind on the end result as you visualise yourself in that relationship, working in your dream place, living the life that you dream of. As you build up a more positive image in your head of what you do want and choose to focus less on what you fear, you will feel as though you've shifted gear in your mind, moving your life forward and away from any fearful thoughts.

Changing your thoughts, your perception and outlook could change your life. Everyone is unique, valuable and worthy. The more you believe it and the more you do to encourage your self-belief, the more confidence you will create, feel and experience in your life.

All these insights and tools from Kamran are brilliant for easing anxiety and finding more peace of mind. I've tried them and they really do work. There's so much you can do to change a pattern of anxiety. And there's no better example of this than Emma, a friend of mine who felt that anxiety was ruining her life.

Emma is a lovely, warm and generous person, but she's always been a bit of a worrier. After she was mugged five years ago, though, her anxiety began to spiral out of control.

She was 24 and she had just landed a new job as a PA to a company director. Emma was thrilled. But it meant a long journey to work and when she had to work late she had to do the long walk from the station to her flat in the dark. One evening, around 9pm, as she walked along the almost-deserted street, she was grabbed from behind. Her bag was wrenched off her shoulder and Emma was pushed to the ground. She got to her feet in time to see her attacker running off down the street.

Emma was badly shaken. She felt bruised and battered and she'd lost her bag with everything in it – purse, keys and phone. She went into a pub, where they let her phone her boyfriend, who came to meet her with a spare key for her flat. And once she got home she had to phone and cancel all her credit cards.

Phones and credit cards can be replaced and bruises heal, but what isn't so easily recovered is peace of mind. Emma had been badly frightened and she became very anxious. She took taxis to and from the station after that, and six months later she moved to another area. But no matter what she did, she didn't feel safe. Her anxiety extended to other things, too. She began to worry about her family and friends, her job and her health. She began constantly checking – had she switched off the iron, the gas, the electric fire? Had she double-locked her door, checked her smoke alarm, put the window catches on? Emma worried so constantly that it was affecting her health.

It was her boyfriend who sat her down and said she had to do something. Her anxiety was changing her personality and affecting their relationship. Emma was shocked – but she realised he was right. She decided to do something about it and she began looking around for possible solutions.

Emma decided to start simply, with ten minutes twice a day spent quietly deep breathing. She also practised the relaxation exercise and made herself a motivational message, one that told herself she was safe in the world and could go out and about with confidence. She also started going to a local yoga class.

It took a few weeks, but Emma began to notice a real difference – and so did her boyfriend. She was calmer and her old confidence was returning. She stopped her constant checking and worrying and began to feel that life was good again.

The thing about anxiety is that if you feed it, it grows. What I mean is, if you focus on the anxiety, and give in to anxious behaviour like needless re-checking, then it gets worse. It's much better to feed your confidence instead, through exercises and practices that help you to feel trusting and calm.

Meditation

I always think meditation sounds like hard work – all that sitting cross-legged focusing on a lotus leaf and emptying your mind. Except that it isn't necessarily like that at all.

Remember Jordan Bone, the girl I mentioned in Chapter 1?

At the age of 15 Jordan was in a car accident and she was left paralysed from the chest down, with limited movement in her fingers. For a while she couldn't see any future for herself at all, but what turned it around for her was – meditation.

'I know it seems unlikely,' Jordan says. 'I was a typical chatty teenager, the last thing I thought about was meditation. But after the accident I felt very low. I wasn't sure what I was going to do with my life. I had a computer and one day I came across a meditation on YouTube. I had nothing else to do, so I tried it, and I really liked it – it made me feel a lot better. I went back to it the next day and the next and after a while I began to see things differently and to feel that maybe there were things I could do.'

Jordan, as you know, went on to start her beauty blog, which is now hugely successful.

As for the meditations, I've had a look myself and there are some really lovely, very short and simple ones on YouTube. And they really do help you to feel less anxious and more peaceful and calm.

The nice thing about a guided meditation is that you have someone talking you through it – which is much easier than just trying to meditate alone.

It's worth persisting with meditation, even if you don't find it easy to switch off – because of all the proven benefits of it. It's been shown to lower your anxiety levels, improve your concentration and help you become more resilient in stressful situations. There are benefits beyond the psychological, too; meditation can help lower high blood pressure and strengthen the immune system. In fact, there is nothing else you can do each day that takes under 20 minutes and has so many profound benefits.

It might just be worth having a go, don't you think?

And finally, here are some of my tried and tested tips that really do help with reducing anxiety and building peace of mind:

- Forgive someone who hurt you. Especially if they didn't mean to.
- Don't read too many newspapers or watch TV news – so much of it is negative.
- Get up and dance round the room to crazy music.
- Go for a walk and photograph beautiful things.
- Don't dwell on the past. Let go of what you can't change and look forward.
- Call an old friend for a long chat.
- Think about what you're grateful for in life.
- Stop taking things personally.
- Do something kind for someone else.
- Play with a friend's child, a niece or nephew.

The more peace of mind you can find for yourself, the calmer and more comfortable your outer world will be. The world we create for ourselves, in our surroundings, is a reflection of what is going on inside us. Chaos inside means chaos outside; and peace inside means a peaceful, happy and confident world around you.

CHAPTER 12

Mentoring

I'm a great believer in the power of mentoring. When I was at my lowest, a mentor really helped me, and through the Foundation I now mentor others.

Mentoring is basically a voluntary relationship in which one person supports, advises and encourages the other. Usually it's someone with a bit more knowledge or experience in a certain area helping someone with a bit less knowledge or experience.

Mentoring can give a fantastic boost to your confidence levels, whichever side of the mentoring relationship you are on, because whether you're sharing experience in a way that will help someone else, or gaining experience, you will feel more confident.

My mentor helped me to come to terms with what had happened to me, and I now do the same for those who have suffered burns and are still adjusting to their situation and who need to find ways to move forward.

I think we can all benefit from being mentored as well as from mentoring someone else. It's a lovely 'pass it on' situation; you learn, and you help someone else to as well, because we've all got experience in some areas of life and there's always someone out there who could benefit from that. And it works the other way round, too – what are you struggling with? Whatever it is, someone out there who has already been through it can probably help.

The basis of mentoring is generosity – wanting to help someone else, simply because you can. So find yourself a mentor – and be one, too.

What is Mentoring?

Mentoring is a way of helping people achieve their potential. It's when one person supports another, passing on what they've learned to help the other person's long-term development. The idea is to help all of us maximise our potential.

It isn't therapy – that's a more formal arrangement in which a trained therapist is paid by the client. Mentoring doesn't usually involve the exchange of money; it is informal and flexible – you might meet a mentor a couple of times, or regularly over years.

The subject of mentoring can be anything – recovery, as in my case – or a dozen other subjects, including success at work, finding work, parenting, mental health, personal development, sports and so on.

Although it's popular now, mentoring isn't new – it's something that has always gone on, although you hear about it more these days. A mentor has often been an older person supporting a younger one, but that's not necessarily true any more. It's more to do with experience and being able to listen to the other person and be honest with them in exchanging ideas, perspectives and what you have learned.

The term mentor comes from a Greek myth. When Odysseus, the Greek King of Ithaca, left to fight in the 10-year Trojan War he left his old friend Mentor in charge of his household and young son Telemachus. Mentor helped to bring up Telemachus and was a loyal friend and advisor to Odysseus, in a relationship built on affection and trust.

Many famous people have relied on mentors. Mark Zuckerberg, who founded Facebook, was mentored by Steve Jobs, former Chief Executive Officer of Apple. When Steve died in 2015, Mark posted on his Facebook page: 'Steve, thank you for being a mentor and friend. Thanks for showing that what you build can change the world. I will miss you.'

Christian Dior mentored Yves St Laurent, who said: 'Dior taught me the basis of my art. I never forgot the years I spent at his side. Richard Branson was mentored by airline entrepreneur Freddie Laker and later said: 'I would never have got anywhere in the airline industry without his help.'

Other fascinating mentor relationships – Bob Dylan mentored singer Jewel, comedian Chris Rock mentored fellow comic Aziz Ansari, Tina Turner was mentor to Mick Jagger, David Cameron's mentor was senior Conservative Michael Howard, Beyonce mentored Rihanna and Rita Ora, and Olympic gold-medal-winner Jessica Ennis mentors young athlete Emelia Gorecka.

None of these were formal mentoring relationships and none involved sitting in meetings. Most of them were friendships that developed naturally into mentoring relationships.

Everyone who has achieved success in what they set out to do has done it with the help of others, people who offered support and advice along the way. And that mentoring is then passed on down the line, to others still hoping to succeed.

My Mentor

The woman who became my mentor, Pam Warren, had survived the Paddington rail crash and recovered from serious burns.

Pam had been a financial advisor, happily married, 32 years old and very successful when she boarded the London-bound train at Reading on the morning of 5 October 1999. At just after 8am the train crashed into another coming the opposite way, and a fireball ripped through the carriages. Thirty-one people died and over 500 were injured, Pam among them.

Pam's burns, to her hands, legs and face, were so bad that she was not expected to survive, and her family were told to prepare for the worst. She did survive, but she needed numerous skin grafts and for 18 months she had to wear a plastic mask, to minimise scarring and infection to the grafts on her face. Pam became the public face of the survivors, known as 'the lady in the mask' and she began campaigning to improve rail safety. But she was also suffering from Post Traumatic Stress Disorder (PTSD) and she began drinking heavily.

In her book, *Behind the Mask*, Pam said, 'After I had stopped taking morphine I found myself replacing its soothing qualities with booze. I began to use alcohol as a way to try to forget the past and to blot out the nightmares. I was becoming a binge-drinker with a serious problem and my marriage started to fall apart.'

Eventually, after months of drunken despair, Pam made the

decision to stop drinking, and for a year she didn't touch a drop. Pam threw herself into campaigning, became an ambassador for Healing Foundation – which supports people living with disfigurement. She also became a hugely successful motivational and business speaker, and a mentor.

It was my brother who contacted Pam on my behalf and asked her to visit me. At that point I was feeling very sorry for myself and I had no idea what I was going to do. My parents and friends were telling me that I was still pretty and that I would meet someone and find a job, but what they were saying didn't mean much to me. 'What did they know?' I thought. I was the one who was burned and had been through hell and as far as I was concerned my life was effectively over.

Pam came to see me and I liked her straight away. She was very straight with me, she didn't pretend everything was fine, but she did tell me there was a way through. And I had to listen to her, because, unlike everyone else, she had been through an ordeal similar to mine. She had worn a mask like the one I had to wear and she'd had some of her fingertips amputated and been through numerous surgeries and yet here she was, with a business and a boyfriend, campaigning and doing charity work and making time to come and see me.

Pam spoke to me in a very straightforward way about her experience of having an adult relationship, meeting people, setting up a business and being a CEO. It was a defining moment in my life. I couldn't argue with her and say that all those things weren't possible for me, because she was living proof that they were possible.

Meeting Pam was a turning point for me – it was the beginning of my decision not to feel sorry for myself and to make the best life I possibly could. Pam had herself been mentored by Simon Weston, who was in the Welsh Guards when his ship, the *Sir Galahad*, was bombed during the Falklands War in 1982. Simon was left badly burned and as he went through numerous grafts and procedures to rebuild his face he also began drinking heavily. But he went on to do a huge amount of charity work and to become a well-known personality on TV and radio.

So Simon mentored Pam, and she mentored me, and I began mentoring other burns' survivors a few years later through the Katie Piper Foundation.

I do have other mentors, too, though they don't always know it. They're people I admire and can learn from, people who I feel are great role models or who have skills I'd love to learn. I get a lot out of spending time with them, seeing what they do and how they do it.

Being a Mentor

Through the Foundation I offer one-to-one mentoring to those who feel they could benefit from it. I see perhaps 20 people a month who have been burned and who are somewhere along the path to recovery. Often it's people who have only recently come out of hospital and who feel that they have no idea what to do next. They may have lost their job, partner, home or all of these, and they will also be dealing with pain, scarring and ongoing medical procedures.

I never tell them that everything is going to be all right in a 'pat them on the head' kind of way. I don't think it would be right to do that because it isn't helpful. Instead I listen to their concerns and I tell them that there is a way forward, based on their physical and mental treatment plan. I tell them that it will take time, but they can make choices about the way they cope and come through what has happened. Sometimes awful things happen and that can open other doors and paths.

In the beginning most of the people I see are, not surprisingly, struggling with all that life has thrown at them. So often people say, 'Why did it happen to me?' They were getting on with a normal life and then had a car crash, or an accident at work or some other event that came out of the blue, and now they have injuries and scars and so much to come to terms with. But I do think that you don't know what the alternatives were. Maybe the thing that happened to you isn't the worst thing, maybe it prevented something worse.

But people do move forward, they see others around them who have done it and they know that it's possible. It's not instant, though, there's no magic wand. It's a question of hard work and determination, one foot in front of the next.

The people I mentor know from the start it's going to be a hard process and I don't pretend that it isn't. I'm usually led by the person, who might have a particular reason to see me, or a list of questions they want to ask, or simply want to tell their story. Others don't want to talk about what has happened to them, they would rather talk about the future. We share experiences and I listen and tell them what worked for me, and what didn't. On the practical side, there are often services, treatment or support that they would benefit from but can't access because of finance or fears or problems with transport, and that's where the Foundation can help. We can do a lot of practical things, like helping to fund transport. We can also offer a specialist make-up session if they don't feel they want to go to a department store counter.

I talk to them about what they want, the real choices that they have and how to manage things day to day, and as I see them start to flourish I know that eventually they will see things very differently and many will become mentors themselves, in five or ten years.

Mentoring people who are traumatised is so worthwhile and I wouldn't change it, but it does take its toll, so I'm always under supervision with a professional supervisor to talk things over with and to give me support, too. These things always work best as a chain, passing on support.

I see people now that I've mentored for years, and they've got their lives together, made new careers, found partners, had kids, and it's wonderful to see; I feel so proud of all of them. What they prove is that in life you fall down many times, but what really matters is getting back up.

A New Direction – Will's Story

Will was 26 when he crashed his motorbike. Bikes can be so invisible on the road, and Will had to swerve to avoid a truck coming straight at him. His bike burst into flames and Will was burned over 40 per cent of his body.

He came to the Foundation six months after the accident and just a few weeks after his release from hospital. When I first met him for a mentoring session Will was angry. He had lost his job as a despatch rider, his flat, his girlfriend – something that often happens as couples struggle to adapt to the new circumstances – and he felt he had very little to live for. He would need several more operations and was still in a lot of pain, and he would always have scarring – over his arm, leg, chest and one side of his face.

Will felt bitter towards the truck driver, which was understandable, as the driver had been at fault. But staying angry wasn't going to help Will, he needed to get his feelings out, to someone who understood, and so for our first couple of meetings I simply listened.

Will was so focused on what had happened that he couldn't think about anything else. But gradually he began to realise that he would have to face the future. He was back living with his mum, spending his days sitting around, so he was bored and lonely. But it was daunting to think that he was going to have to start all over again, by finding a job, and then a place to live, and eventually a relationship.

It felt like a mountain to climb, but Will started by attending a couple of workshops at the Foundation. Meeting others in a similar situation helped, as it nearly always does, and so did doing something creative, like cookery.

A few weeks later Will joined an art class. He loved being absorbed in painting, it took his mind away from his troubles and over the next few months he began to feel more positive about the future. But he still didn't know what job he was going to do. Although he hadn't planned to be a despatch rider forever, he had enjoyed it. He loved being out in the open and moving around – sitting behind a desk was his idea of a nightmare. While he thought about what to do he began helping an elderly neighbour with her garden. It was a mess; she hadn't been able to manage it for a few years, so Will set himself the challenge of making it beautiful again. And to his surprise, he loved it. The physical exercise, the open air and the creativity of planning and making the garden lifted his spirits and made him feel that life just might be worthwhile again.

Two years on, Will is a successful landscape gardener with his own business. He spends his days outdoors and he looks tanned and well. His life has purpose again, and he is dating one of his gardening clients.

Mentoring didn't fix things for Will, he did that for himself, but it offered him support, information and encouragement while he found his way through all the confusion and strangeness of life after a major accident.

It makes me happy to have helped him. What happened to me was terrible but being able to mentor people like Will is one of the positives that have come out of it.

Find a Mentor

If you think that you might benefit from having a mentor there are plenty of ways to find one. You can go through a charity, if you have a link to one (many charities offer mentors) or you can use some of the great websites that offer mentors – look online and you'll see there are some excellent websites offering carefully vetted mentors for everything from parenting to managing your finances.

You might also look around you for a mentor – is there someone you already know and respect whose support or expertise might help you?

The key to being mentored is to find someone you think highly of and whom you can learn from, either by talking to them or by watching what they do. Look at how they do things and learn from it. Let your role models guide you, and pass on that information, by guiding and helping others.

Most people love being asked for advice, so if you decide to approach someone for an informal mentoring relationship it can be as simple as inviting them for a coffee or asking for a bit of information.

You may come to a practical arrangement with your mentor, meeting or speaking regularly to update on your progress and talk over next steps. But it's also possible to see someone as a mentor without telling them. I have several men and women who mentor me without even knowing it – lawyers, business people, psychologists and people in the world of books have all been role models for me as I re-defined my life and set up the Foundation. I respect them and I learn from them, copying techniques, ideas and skills.

If you think about it, everybody is someone else's role model; we're all living someone else's dream. That's why mentoring is such a great thing, because you can choose a mentor and you can be one, too.

You may think your life couldn't be anyone else's dream, but think for a minute. When I was in intensive care, my dream was to get out. So the people already out, starting their lives again, were my role models. And when I was recovering but on disability benefits, with no job, the person who had just landed a job was my role model.

Now I've been able to do things that were on somebody else's list of what they wanted to achieve. That's how it works. So don't envy other people who seem to have achieved so much more than you have, in whatever way – learn from them and do what they do.

To make mentoring work, you need to:
- Be willing to step out of your comfort zone and try something new, or in a different way.
- Respect your mentor and listen to what they say.
- Work hard at making the changes you need to make and learning the skills you want.
- Be tough with yourself, at times. Don't always go for the easy route.
- Stick with it for long enough to see a difference.

Be a Mentor

Who is a mentor? It is simply someone who has lived and learned and can pass on some of that learning in a friendly, supportive way.

You may think you don't have what it takes to be a mentor, but perhaps you do. Because there is almost certainly something you know about, or have managed or achieved that someone else might benefit from.

Mentoring is a great way to give something back, to share what you have and to begin a meaningful relationship with someone else.

If you've had difficulties or overcome problems, it makes you an even better mentor. Kids who have lost direction, or got into trouble with petty crime and drugs, are often successfully mentored by someone who has been there, done it and come out the other side. Those with a drink problem who join Alcoholics Anonymous are sponsored – or mentored – by a member who is further ahead on the sobriety path. And someone starting out in a business is often mentored by an older colleague, who keeps a friendly eye on their progress and offers advice when it is needed.

Living with a long-term condition is another area in which a mentor can be such a help. Someone who has just been diagnosed with chronic fatigue syndrome, or arthritis, or diabetes, may feel overwhelmed by the prospect of coping. But a mentor who has managed the condition for some years can help them navigate through the early days.

Whether it's for the short term or the long term, mentoring is so valuable. For someone being bullied, going through redundancy or job loss, struggling to find a job or to overcome an addiction, it can mean a lifeline.

You might think, well, why should I bother? What do I get out of mentoring? Well, actually, such a lot. Mentoring someone gives you the pleasure of sharing what you know, seeing someone benefit from your advice and making a connection with someone that is valuable for both of you. It's great for your self-esteem because it reminds you of your own value. You get to see yourself through someone else's eyes – someone who appreciates and respects you.

In case you were thinking that you're too young to be a mentor, you don't have to be old. You can mentor someone at any age. Older teenagers in school mentor younger ones. People in their early twenties have all kinds of life experience they can pass on. And mentoring, apart from all the other benefits, can improve your life-skills, such as listening and problem-solving.

To make being a mentor work you need to:

- Want to help someone.
- Recognise just how much you know.
- Polish life-skills like listening and problem-solving.
- Avoid trying to fix the other person – they'll do that, you just need to support them.
- Encourage the person you're mentoring to push their boundaries.

If there's one skill that's absolutely vital to mentoring, it's listening. Sounds simple, but it can actually be quite a challenge to listen to someone without interrupting, and without losing concentration. To really hear what they are saying, and sometimes what they're not saying, too, you need to be an active listener, and that does take practice. Most of us are used to conversations where we talk over each other, butt in, zone out and forget what the other person just said. Active listening isn't like that, it's a real skill and it's a great thing to be able to do it – useful for all kinds of situations in life.

Practise whenever you can. Next time someone is talking to you, focus on what they're saying and just listen. Don't interrupt, say mmm or fiddle with your bag/phone/keys. Just listen as though you've got to be able to repeat back to the person what they just said. That way you actually take in what they are saying. Keep the pause button on your response until you are certain the person has finished. Then if you aren't certain about any aspect of what they've said, you can ask. Sometimes it actually does help to repeat back all or part of what the person said.

For the other person this can be a very uplifting experience. It's not often that we feel really heard, and as though what we have to say is valid and matters.

No matter what else you bring to the table, if you become a good listener you will be a good mentor.

Mentoring is a win-win situation; you both benefit in all kinds of ways, not least in a boost to your self-esteem. And you both come away feeling enriched by a relationship that has been all about moving forward and positive outcomes.

Mentor Yourself

If you can't find a mentor or don't feel that you want to talk to someone else in a traditional mentoring situation, then self-mentoring is the way to go. You may have doubts about this approach, but it really does work, because inside each of us, no matter how low, uncertain, inexperienced or unsure we feel, is a wise, thoughtful self whom we can turn to.

Self-mentoring means really getting to know yourself. It means taking responsibility for your own development and progress and using your initiative to make decisions, take up opportunities and move forward.

If you're going to self-mentor then it's a good idea to start by identifying your own strengths, weaknesses, needs, values, passions and how you might respond in various situations. You need to know what matters to you, what you want and what fires you up.

The SWOT Test

SWOT stands for Strengths, Weaknesses, Opportunities and Threats, and this is a little test that's been around for some time. It's really useful, lots of businesses use it, and you can do your own little SWOT test to start off your self-mentoring programme, using my version.

So grab a pen and a piece of paper and answer these questions:

Strengths

What are you naturally good at?

What skills do you have?

What might other people see as your strengths?

What are your values?

What have you done in the past that you're really proud of?

Weaknesses

What do you put off doing or prefer to avoid?

What could you improve?

Where in your life do you lack confidence?

What might other people see as your weaknesses?

What training or education might benefit you?

Opportunities

What would you like to be doing with your life?

Is there a demand for a skill or ability that you have?

Would you be willing to re-train?

Would you like to start your own business?

Do you know people who might be helpful to you in moving forward?

Threats

What obstacles are you facing?

Are you holding yourself back?

Are you avoiding something you know you can do to help yourself?

Is anyone around you holding you back?

Are you afraid of going for what you want?

Once you've answered everything, look at what is emerging. You will probably find a pattern, a few clues and a few things to set you thinking. You can add to what you've written if you think of more answers – the idea is to get as full a picture as possible of who you are, what you love doing and what might be right for you. This test works whether you're thinking about work, finding a relationship or what do with your spare time.

Once you've got the answers, you can begin to start making a plan to move yourself forward. I find this TASK reminder is really helpful:

- Take one step forward each day, no matter how small.
- Action – what do you need to do to achieve your outcome?
- Support – look around for the people who will help, support and encourage you.
- Knowledge – what do you need to find out, from books, people, the internet?

And finally don't forget about encouragement – give yourself lots of positive self-talk, remind yourself that you are capable of so much; you have so much more in you than you realise and amazing things are possible.

If you're self-mentoring, look on everything that happens as a mentoring possibility, and everyone you meet as a possible mentor. There's almost always something we can learn from others that will help us towards our goals. Be on the lookout for ideas to pursue, tips and opportunities to put yourself into new situations. Don't dismiss anything unless you've tried it and don't pass up any potential resources.

The Value of Mentoring

Whatever route you choose, whether you're looking for a mentor, thinking about becoming one or even self-mentoring, take the opportunity to use mentoring as a way of moving your life forward and discovering new possibilities, inside you and around you. We're not in this world to do things alone – we need other people and so many of them are willing to help us, if we ask them. Mentors have made a big difference in my life – let them do the same for you.

CHAPTER

Acceptance

Acceptance is what happens when we let go and recognise things just as they are, instead of struggling to change them, wishing they were different or resenting them. It can be tough to accept a situation that makes us unhappy, but when we can't change it, acceptance is the only way to find peace of mind, and to begin to move forward.

Many of us struggle with self-acceptance, too. Learning to accept yourself is a big challenge, but it will reap huge rewards, because when you accept yourself, others will sense it and accept you, too. Self-acceptance is tangible, you know when you come across someone who feels comfortable in their own skin; they tend to be calm, easy to be around and full of humour and confidence. Who wouldn't want to be like that?

After all, it's hard work looking for approval, or trying to make everyone like you. And it's a relief to give it up, I can promise you that. Confident people accept it when someone doesn't like them.

206

They know that it's impossible to be liked by everyone, and that often when someone doesn't like you, it says more about them than about you.

Finding acceptance is a choice, and it's one worth making because with acceptance you feel calmer and happier and life feels more straightforward. It's only when you accept yourself that others begin to accept you, too. It's like a domino effect, and it all starts with you.

It was a difficult journey for me to get to a place where I could accept what had happened to me. I wanted to fight it with everything I had, but I couldn't. It was better to put all that angry energy into accepting the facts and learning to live with them. You have to live the life you have, with whatever you've been given. And once you accept that, you can focus on making the absolute best of what you do have.

For me, finding acceptance was like cracking a secret code. I couldn't believe the difference it made to me and to my life. Acceptance is so different from resignation; resigning yourself to something is depressing, but acceptance carries with it a lot of hope. When you accept, you free yourself to start moving on.

Acceptance doesn't happen overnight, whether that's self-acceptance or acceptance of a situation in your life. But there's a lot you can do to speed up the process and move on. So in this chapter I will outline steps you can take every day, to make self-acceptance, and acceptance of your life situation and of others, too, a part of your life. Because acceptance is the foundation stone of confidence.

Self-Acceptance

Self-acceptance is being happy with who you are, and how you are, right now. It doesn't mean that you might not want to change things in the future; it just means that, at this moment, you're fine with yourself. It's a way of coming to terms with whatever has troubled you – that might be a disability, a scar, a condition, or it might be something about your body, face or hair. It might also be something about yourself – something that you perceive to be wrong or bad. Maybe you didn't pass an exam or you can't drive or you don't get jokes. It could be anything, because that's what we do – pick on something about ourselves that we think is not good enough and then feel bad because if it, even though we can't change it. It's a lose-lose situation. On the other hand, saying, 'Well, that's just how it is, and how I am' can be such a relief. No more fretting or wondering why. It's just how it is! Maybe there's no more to it than that.

Think of yourself as though you were your home. It might not be perfect, but it's where you live right now. You might want to make some improvements in the future, or change a few things or even move to another home, but at this moment it's fine just as it is.

We have to engage with the life we have and with who we are – even if life throws the unexpected at us. A lemon we didn't see coming . . . But there's no need to make that all about something you did wrong. I was chatting to someone recently who had a child with a genetic disease. She told me, 'For the longest time I blamed myself, because I passed on the DNA containing the disease. I felt so bad. But in the end I realised – I hadn't known! How could it be my fault? It was just what happened. I won't even say it was bad luck, because I wouldn't change anything about my child, she's perfect just as she is.' Brave words, and so true. Something that seems heartbreaking and awful so often contains a blessing. Which is all the more reason then to accept what we have and work with it, not against it. We can find meaning and joy in our experiences of difficulties.

We can't choose our differences, or those of the people we love. We can only accept them and learn to love them. And while we do, we have to accept that not everyone will like or accept us. That's something I've had to come to terms with. There is an affirmation that I used to have written down in my flat when I lived by myself – 'I am what I am and that's not that bad'. I put it above my front door and would see it every time I went out and it helped me to keep things in perspective.

Acceptance from Others

It can be very tough to have something about you that others find hard to accept. Even families, those closest to us, can struggle with acceptance. They might love us, but that doesn't mean they accept everything about us.

Sometimes it takes time. Plenty of people have told their families something which at first shocked them, only to find that, with time, acceptance came. I have a good friend who put off for many years telling his parents he was gay, because they came from a very different culture in which being gay hadn't yet become accepted. When he did finally tell them they were stunned and he thought he'd done the wrong thing. But, six months on, first his mother and then his father accepted the situation, because they loved him. Now he's planning a wedding, and his parents will be there. So if you're looking for acceptance, go gently, give it time, and make sure that you accept yourself before you look for acceptance from others.

As a society we're becoming kinder and more accepting. Conditions such as Down's Syndrome, for instance, used to result in appalling prejudice and ill-treatment. Those with the condition were put away in homes and considered not to be 'a person'. Since then there has been a radical change in attitude. People with Down's take part in all areas of life, many live independently and the public perception is so much warmer, kinder and more tolerant.

So acceptance is on the increase, and that's great news. But there's still a way to go. I would like to see more acceptance of those with scarring. It's one of the last taboos – people still think it's OK to wear fake scars on Halloween to scare people and that makes me mad – why should that be OK? It gives a terrible message. I'm trying to teach my daughter not to be frightened of people with burns, so the last thing I want is to see people dressing up in fake scars. Better to stick to cats and pumpkins.

The great thing about acceptance is that it brings out the best in us – kindness, cheerfulness, warmth towards one another. These are the things we all need more of.

An Acceptance Exercise

This is a simple exercise that is really useful in learning to accept your situation. It's all about what is happening, in this moment, rather than what has been or might be.

You can do this exercise alone or with someone else.

Sit in a chair and make yourself comfortable. Then ask yourself the following questions and give the answers out loud. Saying it makes it more real.

What are my feelings at the moment?
Describe what you feel. For instance, I am feeling happy, sad, angry, frustrated, disappointed and so on. Keep going until you have named all your current feelings.

What are my sensations at the moment?
Describe what is going on in your body. For instance, my foot hurts, there's an itch on my arm, I'm warm – or cold, I'm hungry . . . Keep going until you've described everything you are sensing in this moment.

What is going on outside my body at the moment?
Describe what is happening around you. For instance, is it light or dark? What can you see through the window, is the sun shining? What is there in the room? Is the door open or shut? And so on. Do it without making any judgement about whether something is good or bad, or wishing it was different. For instance, if it's cold, notice the cold without wishing you could turn the heat up.

This exercise helps to ground us in the moment, to remind us of what is, rather than what is not, and in that there is the possibility of finding acceptance. If you start by accepting how you feel right now, it's the first step to accepting the bigger picture.

Accepting the End of a Relationship

A counsellor once told me that though she sees clients with a wide range of problems – depression, anxiety, stress, poor self-esteem and so on – the vast majority of them embark on therapy because of a relationship problem. In other words, although they may have long-standing issues, it's usually current romantic difficulties that drive them to seek help at that time.

I can understand that. Finding someone to love is a Number One priority for most of us. And obviously when a relationship fails, we feel terribly upset.

When we are distressed in that way, we do consider therapy, and of course we often buy a book that we hope will help us get over our pain and inspire us. So it's quite possible that you might have picked up this book because you recently suffered a relationship break-up which has left you feeling pretty low. If so, please take comfort from the fact that you are not alone.

This is not a book on getting over heartbreak – there are plenty of those around – but I think this chapter would be a good place to learn a little bit about accepting yourself and regaining confidence when you are newly single. It's a tough time and most of us have been there – often more than once!

The fact is that if you're going to really begin to live again after a failed love affair, you need to do a lot of accepting. You have to accept that the relationship really is over and that though you will love again, and be loved, it won't be with that same person. That's the first thing. Secondly, you need to accept yourself as someone who is now – and temporarily – single again. Both of these things are harder than they sound.

In the wake of a relationship split, who hasn't said: 'He doesn't know his own mind.' Or: 'She'll never manage without me.' Or: 'He'll realise his mistake'? I know I've said these things. It's also easy to think, 'Of course she didn't love me, no one would' or 'I'm not worthy of love.' But I also know that you don't get over your heartache while you think like that. So you need to let yourself feel the whole weight of the sorrow that the relationship really is over before your new life can start. And during that period you need to be comforted and helped by people who love you.

Unfortunately, not everyone will unconditionally love and support you at this time. Perhaps some members of your family have hinted that the end of the relationship is your fault. That can be very hard. I have a friend – let's call her Jilly – whose mum is desperate for her daughter to find Mr Right and start producing a family so she can become a granny. When Jilly's boyfriend dumped her recently, her mum was not at all helpful. Instead, she kept moaning on about how at this rate all her friends would be grandparents and she would be left behind. She also implied that her daughter was 'impossible' and that her boyfriend was right to dump her. How unkind is that?

We all need love and support as we go through that acceptance phase and if you're not getting it from your family, make sure you get it from your friends.

It's important, too, not just to accept the *situation*, but also to accept *yourself* as a single-again person. It may be that you don't want to see yourself in that light, having preferred to think of yourself as part of a couple. But you honestly won't get over your break-up unless you do some real self-acceptance. By the way, this may involve careful self-examination – which can be hard.

In Jilly's case, her mother's comments made her look carefully at herself and at how she'd behaved in the relationship. And she then admitted to me that she had been a bit argumentative and clingy in it, which had driven her boyfriend mad. We talked some more, and it turned out that she was still upset about being dumped by a *previous* man and that had made her very insecure – and because of that, she'd jumped straight into another relationship.

So, my advice to her was to have six months learning to be herself again and to enjoy being single before even thinking about being with someone new. Pushing your feelings aside and simply replacing one partner for another is crazy. You can become seriously mixed up.

Jilly has now decided to use this new 'single' time to work for a higher qualification so that she can go for a promotion. She is also planning a holiday with some girlfriends and she's embarked on a healthy eating programme.

All these things seem good to me because they suggest that she is accepting her new life and taking responsibility for improving her job prospects and for having a good time.

That's not to say she won't sometimes wish she was still in her recent relationship but she has accepted that it's over and that she is going to use her single time till the next partner turns up to live as vibrantly and as productively as possible. I'm proud of her!

I am also pleased that she is looking at what she regrets about her own behaviour in the recent relationship. And in her case, because she never got over the man before the most recent one, she knows she tended to act rather hysterically at times. She is accepting that – and that is good.

People with good mental health know the difference between

having healthy regard and acceptance for *themselves* but, at the same time, resolving to alter their *behaviour* when it has been poor or unhelpful.

Who hasn't got a few things in their past that they now regret? I know I have. But our mistakes should not affect our total acceptance and love of ourselves as a whole.

Accepting Ill Health and Loss

A few years ago my mum got cancer. It was hard to believe that my brilliant, loving mum, after caring for me, nursing and supporting me all the way through the first years of my recovery, had got cancer. It just wasn't fair.

My family were such a big part of my recovery. I couldn't have come through it all without them. After I left hospital they took me home and Mum took time off from her job as a classroom special needs assistant to care for me. She and my dad, who is a barber, helped me through my physiotherapy four times a day, fed, bathed and nursed me. They got me back on my feet, and then out of the house and, along with my little sister Susie and my big brother Paul, they were in my corner, loving me, encouraging me and believing in me day after day.

So the news, a couple of years ago, that Mum had bowel cancer was heartbreaking. Mum has seen me go through so much, and now she was beginning her own health ordeal. She had surgery and then chemotherapy and the cancer seemed to have gone, but then it came back, this time as a secondary cancer in her liver. Once again she had surgery, and chemo, and once again it seemed to have gone, but back it came and she needed further surgery on

215

her liver. Thankfully the liver regenerates, and so far things look good – Mum has had clear scans and she's back at work.

It was incredibly hard for me, and I think for all of our family, to accept Mum's illness. It seemed so unfair, but the honest truth is that once you're over the age of seven there's no point in saying that anything in life is unfair. Life just comes along, bringing the good and the bad, and you have to deal with both.

Learning to accept something like the illness – and potential loss – of someone you love is so hard. But part of accepting what has happened is realising how precious they are and valuing every moment together.

These days I Facetime my mother most days so that she can see Belle. Mum adores her granddaughter; Belle has brought beauty into my parents' lives. After the attack Mum and Dad were left with the memory of walking into an intensive care ward to see me in a coma. But then a new memory was created, when they walked into my hospital room just after I had given birth to Belle.

Building new, positive memories helps so much. I had to accept that Mum had cancer, just as she had to accept what happened to me. But now we collect good things – good memories and good things in life, like wonderful experiences, travel, friends and better health.

I also rely on learning so much from other people about how to accept, with a smile, what life brings us. One of them is Vicky Kuhn, an amazing woman who joined our Disability Catwalk at the Ideal Home Show in 2015. Vicky is in a wheelchair, but she hasn't let that stop her leading a full and interesting life. There isn't a hint of self-pity about her, Vicky is someone who has accepted life as it is, and then made the absolute most of it.

I'll let her tell you her story in her own words.

My Army of Warriors – Vicky's Story

2015 was the year when I stopped mourning for what could have been and started accepting life as a disabled woman.

It had been several years since I'd been diagnosed with Ehlers-Danlos Syndrome. I know, it's a mouthful and no one's ever heard of it. It's pretty rare, and it's a genetic disorder of the body's connective tissue. It leads to a long list of symptoms, which in my case include difficulties with my feet and legs and a whole host of other problems. Although I had symptoms as a teenager, my condition wasn't diagnosed until I was in my twenties. By that time I'd married, had two children and divorced. So I was coping as a single mum and the news that I had an incurable lifelong condition was absolutely devastating.

Three years ago I could no longer walk, even with a stick, and I had to accept being in a wheelchair. I had refused to accept it for so long that in the end it was a relief, but I still hated it and for a while I felt very down.

It was probably being a mum that forced me to stop feeling sorry for myself and accept my disability. I had always wanted to lead by example and to teach my children that you can do anything you set your mind to. So how could I sit there wallowing in self-pity?

My kids have always been my driving force. It wasn't easy being a single parent with a disability, but my son and daughter are both amazing and they became very independent. As my condition progressed I needed a carer, and that's when I met Jason. He arrived to care for me and now we are married and he supports me in every way. The family grew even bigger, with my three stepchildren, and now we're a big, noisy throng.

217

Stuck at home and unable to go out to work, I started a blog. I called it 'Around and Upside Down'. It's about fashion, beauty, food, travel and . . . life – all from the point of view of a disabled mum. I've always loved fashion and beauty; I love quirky looks, unusual clothes and dressing up. Writing it gave me a sense of purpose, and it got a fantastic response. I got a small army of Twitter followers and I began to feel much more connected to the world outside my home.

Having a plethora of illnesses, resulting in chronic disability, I need to search hard for the things that make me feel good. My family inspire me most of all, and I write about them often. I love good food, and a couple of years ago I started focusing more on healthy choices, as I realised my health was worsening because of weight gained from a few years of making the wrong choices.

Being able to blog and communicate on Twitter gave me an incredible boost. It allowed me to share my views, my silly humour, my passion and my excitement about life with all kinds of people. I didn't expect to get much of a response, I did it for me, really, but now I have a big following and I love it.

The sheer army of warriors I chat with on a regular basis is amazing! These warriors are mums trying to make sense of the delight, diversity and difficulties of parenting a child. These warriors are style gurus, telling us how to apply our war paint. These warriors are intrepid travellers and tasters of the world, enlivening their senses with the rich cities and foods the world has to offer. These warriors are disabled and chronically ill people who share their journeys with us. I fall into all of these categories.

In 2015, at the age of 33, I decided to make it my year of saying yes to everything I was offered or asked to do. I had said no for so long, worried about my disability, but as people began contacting me through the blog and I started saying yes, I realised – you know what, I'm disabled, nothing can change that, but it's OK and life is still good.

Saying yes led me to do some marvellous things – I got involved with Katie's models of diversity catwalk, although for me it was a wheel, not a walk. I loved doing it, so when I was asked to do a fashion shoot with the London College of Fashion, I said yes.

As one thing led to another, life got pretty busy. I became a disabled rights campaigner and began going on training courses.

In the course of a year everything had changed. And that change began with me accepting that I was disabled and deciding that, rather than fighting it and denying it, I would make the best of it. I didn't know then just how good the best could be.

I accepted myself, but being accepted by others when you're in a wheelchair is very hit and miss, in large part because we are not represented in the media. You might get a friendly shop assistant in *Balamory* in a wheelchair, or a clever but dorky cast member in *Glee*. It's a start, but where are the sexy wheelchair-bound vixens in sitcoms? Where are the cheerful disabled children in school dramas? Where are we, the disabled, in politics and public life?

Many people see me as 'just a chair' and talk to the person with me, whether or not I engaged that person in conversation. Others (especially town planners and local councils) forget I exist. Wheelchair users don't need to get around. They don't need to use pavements; they don't want to use public transport. Oh, but we do!

Without the chair, I'm just the same as any other woman. I like to go out, shop for clothes, shop for make-up, wear beautiful clothes and look good.

That's why I love my blog – I love to help educate and inform, to ask questions, to challenge ideas. I am very proud to be part of a new wave of people with disabilities who are ready to stand up and be counted.

And to anyone else in a wheelchair, or disabled in any way, or simply down, depressed, at a loss, I would say shout loud and stand tall. Whatever your disability or difficulty, you are just as good as those who don't have your particular set of problems. Overcome what you can, and live with and work around what you can't. And don't be afraid to ask for help from those who have been there before you.

Acceptance Works

The bottom line with acceptance, if you're asking 'Why should I accept?', is that acceptance works. It brings you peace of mind, helps your self-esteem and leads to a calmer and more confident you. When you accept whatever has come along for you, whether that's the loss of someone you love, something that feels like a failure or a difficult experience, then you let go of all the anger, denial and the wish that things were different. You free up the energy you need to cope and to move forward in life. And you grow as a person, because it takes maturity to accept something when every bit of you wants a different outcome.

When we fight and resist what can't be changed our minds become turbulent and unhappy. When we start to welcome what happens to us, knowing that we will survive it, and perhaps even find blessings in it, then we have found deep, inner confidence.

Acceptance is about being realistic and practical. But it's not weakness, it's strength. It's not resignation, not an unhappy, 'Oh well' attitude, it's a 'This is how it is and I can cope' attitude.

When we know how to accept life, graciously and without fear, then we are prepared for anything. No matter what crisis or difficulty comes along, we can take it in our stride and life will flow smoothly.

CHAPTER 14

Gratitude

We live life in such a rush that we often forget to appreciate the many good things that come to us each day, and the many blessings that exist in our lives. We tend to focus on the problems, the hold-ups and the worries and we take so much for granted – forgetting to appreciate what we have until we lose it.

Being grateful is not just a nice thing to be – it's actually amazingly good for us. By focusing on the positive in our lives we create a sunnier outlook, greater confidence and we become healthier and happier. And most of us have a lot we can be grateful for – from our families to our work and the small things that make up our everyday lives.

It's harder to be grateful for the tough things that come along in life, but if we can get through them, they make us stronger and we can be grateful for that strength, and for what we have learned from coping with difficulty.

Gratitude, practised daily, can become a habit. And it's a great one to have; it makes you stronger, wiser and braver. When you know that there is something to be grateful for in every day, no matter what it brings, then you can let go of fear and welcome change.

So don't take all the good things in your life for granted; count your blessings, be aware of them and enjoy the warm glow that gratitude brings and the confidence that comes from knowing you are lucky and that your life is good.

Gratitude, by the way, is not the same as being indebted. Feeling that you owe someone can be a negative thing, it can be associated with resentment or duty, but true gratitude is a warm and positive feeling unconnected to debt of any kind. So warm that it's catching – if you express gratitude to someone, both you, and they, are likely to have warmer feelings towards others for the rest of the day.

How Gratitude Helped Me

I try to spend a little time every day saying thank you for all that I have in my life, my husband and daughter, my lovely family, my friends and colleagues and my work, my home and all the other things that make my life so rich and blessed – not least the amazing medical staff who look after me whenever I'm in hospital.

Before the attack I took life very much for granted. I had a good life, I was sharing a flat in London and was busy laying the foundations of what I hoped would be an exciting and enjoyable career, while going out and having a lot of fun, so I didn't really think about gratitude.

After the attack, at first I thought only about survival. But as time went on I began to be aware of how grateful I felt – to the doctors who had saved me, and for life itself. I was grateful for any improvement – a bandage off, the drip out of my stomach, being able to smile, getting my eyesight back in one eye. I had taken my health for granted, but now these gradual advances meant the world to me. As I recovered I realised that I would be grateful for whatever life I had, because having come so close to losing life, it felt very precious.

As time went by I began to hope for more. I would think, 'What if I could start driving again? What if I could do some voluntary work? What if I could live independently?'

Each time I achieved one of these goals I gave thanks. I felt so grateful for everything, nothing was automatic any more, every tiny goalpost felt amazing. And although I didn't realise it then, the gratitude I felt was part of my recovery, it helped me to heal, physically and mentally.

Since those days I've always felt enormously grateful for everything that has come my way. I never imagined I would present programmes on TV or write books. And when I did start writing, once I'd told my story it felt natural to want to write a book of affirmations – positive thoughts and messages full of gratitude and appreciation, because I used them all the time. I always keep lovely affirmations and sayings about thankfulness around me, at home and on my phone, they help me through the day and remind me of what matters most.

There have been so many things about my journey of the last few years that I can be thankful for. When I was flat-sharing and trying for a TV career I was taking jobs selling cordless kettles and solar garden lights on shopping channels, or appearing on roulette channels at four in the morning, in front of a single camera and a green screen.

Now I've got the most interesting job I could imagine. I travel and meet fascinating people I really believe in. Channel 4 keep me busy and I'm so grateful for the opportunities they give me, and for the interesting, bright and funny colleagues I get to work with. I find them all inspirational.

And if all the work dried up tomorrow, although I'd be sad, I would be grateful for what I've had and I'd find something else to do. Once you've been through a major trauma you know that what you have can disappear in an instant, and being aware that you could lose it makes you more resilient – you got through it once so you'll get through it again – and more grateful for having what is in your life today.

Because I lost the ability, physically, to work for a few years, having work now means a lot to me, so I put my heart and soul into it. When I couldn't work I felt a bit useless, I lost my identity. That might not be true for everyone, but for me work was important, so now I have work I don't resent it when I have to do it in the evening or at the weekend.

My life over the past nine years has been an extraordinary rollercoaster. When I was wearing the plastic mask I needed to protect and heal the new skin on my face I was thrown out of shops and people called me a freak. So when I wrote my first book I believed it was a story no one would want to hear. And then it sold in 32 countries – in places I had never been to – and translated into languages I had never even heard of. I was stunned, and it helped me to believe that, for every person who is thoughtlessly cruel, there are many, many more who care, who are kind and who want to know the real story. And for that I was, and am, so grateful.

The life I have now is a life I could only dream about when I was very ill. So when Richie says he'd love to win the lottery, I tell him, 'No, you wouldn't, we've got everything we could wish for now.' We have one another and Belle, we live a good life, he has a job he loves and so do I. Winning a lot of money wouldn't add anything to that. So instead of wishing for more, I give thanks for what is, every single day.

The Upside of Gratitude

There isn't just one upside of gratitude – there are dozens! Numerous scientific and psychological studies have proved that the regular practice of gratitude – saying, writing and thinking your thanks – has the most extraordinary effect on our systems.

Among other things, giving thanks:

- Increases our sense of wellbeing, satisfaction and happiness
- Increases our energy
- Makes us more optimistic
- Improves our ability to empathise with others
- Helps us sleep better
- Makes us kinder and more compassionate
- Enhances the immune system
- Calms aggressive and angry feelings.

It always amazes me that something as simple as saying 'thank you' every day can actually benefit your immune system. But it does, and it benefits mental health, too, making us less likely to become depressed, smoke, take drugs, drink heavily or become isolated. Among many other things, gratitude helps us make connections with others.

So don't save your thanks for the day you get promoted or meet the love of your life, give thanks for everything, large and small, every day.

As well as all the other benefits, gratitude has the power to heal us emotionally. Evidence shows that people who practise gratitude find that traumatic memories fade into the background faster, and troubling thoughts become less intense and less frequent. Scientists believe that being thankful actually helps the brain to fully process negative events and make sense of them, in other words, to achieve a sense of completion and put the event behind them.

And other people respond to gratitude. Even a simple 'thank you' spurs people to act in more considerate and kind ways. People thanked for giving directions help more willingly in the future, social workers who get thank-you letters visit their clients more often, and shop assistants who are thanked go the extra mile when it comes to good service. We don't need research to prove this, do we? Because we all know how nice it is to be thanked and how we immediately feel warmer and are prepared to give a bit more.

I can't help feeling that gratitude really is the glue that holds us all together.

Appreciate Happy Moments

So how do we go about being grateful? How do we exercise the gratitude muscle and get all those lovely benefits?

For me, gratitude starts in small steps, and there's no better way than by noticing and appreciating happy moments. This is a practical, common-sense suggestion that everyone can adopt and that really does make a difference. Our grannies probably called this strategy 'counting your blessings', but whatever name you want to give to this goal, all you have to do is look out for happy moments in your day and make a note of at least five of them.

If you do this, you will not only feel more cheerful, you will actually train your brain to 'accentuate the positive', as the old song goes, rather than dwell on everything that has gone wrong in the day.

Here are some of the things that you might notice:

- The cup of coffee you buy on your way to work
- The sun shining
- A passenger smiling at you on the bus
- A positive comment from a colleague
- The satisfaction of getting a job done
- A nice text from a friend
- A hug from your partner.

You can go on from here to appreciate things about your life, things that most of the time we take for granted:

- Your health, and the health of people you love
- Living in a country where you have freedom of speech
- The fact that you met your partner
- Having somewhere safe and warm to live.

Keep a Gratitude Journal

This is an idea that has fast caught on. Taking a few minutes every day to write down the things you are thankful for helps to build up a strong sense of wellbeing. Try to find new things every day, because while writing 'I'm grateful for my job' day after day is not a bad thing, it's noticing new things that really gives us a strong sense of appreciating our lives and the world around us.

Look for those moments that so often pass by quickly and become forgotten. The cup of tea your friend made you because you were upset, the meal your partner made to surprise you, the 'are you all right?' phone call from a parent. All the things that people around us do to show they care are special, so be specific when you write your thanks. Doing this makes you notice things; it opens your eyes and makes life more joyful. And if you're anything like me, once you start looking for things to be grateful for, you can't stop. It becomes like a game, spotting things as you go through your day.

People who start a daily gratitude journal actually change for the better. Others around them report that they become more helpful. And of course once they become more helpful and positive to be around, the effect multiplies; with a positive attitude they're likely to make more friends and that makes them even more thankful, because nothing brings joy like having good friends.

One recent study showed that keeping a brief gratitude journal just once a week, and writing down five things the participants were grateful for each time, had a marked effect on their happiness in just two months.

Another study found that those who kept a gratitude journal

fell asleep more quickly, slept for longer and woke refreshed. So if you want to get a good night's sleep, count blessings, not sheep!

Say Thank You

There's nothing quite like actually thanking another person. All of the benefits of gratitude are multiplied when we express gratitude face-to-face. So who deserves your thanks? Who has shown you kindness and concern, support and caring? Tell them. We often forget to thank the people closest to us, the partner who brings you a morning coffee, the children who brighten your day, the parents who did so much for us as we grew up.

Appreciating people can actually calm inflamed situations. So, next time there's a tense atmosphere at home, or a bit of an argument going on, try to defuse it with thanks. It really can work.

Thank people you encounter every day, in a shop or cafe, on a bus or train, at work and over the phone. If they have helped you in any way, thank them as fully as possible.

You might also feel that you want to thank someone who is not around now. A parent, an old friend, a teacher, coach or supervisor, who really made a difference in your life. Perhaps you haven't seen them for some time, you've lost touch or they live far away. Think about giving them a ring or even writing them a letter of thanks. Tell them what they did for you, and what it meant to you. Imagine how wonderful it would be if you received a letter like that. And it is also a wonderful feeling to write one. Gratitude is a funny thing – once you start feeling grateful it can just pour out, and you remember all kinds of things you appreciate in your life.

You can even write a letter of thanks that you don't send – perhaps to someone you have lost contact with, or even to someone who has died. Or you might want to write to someone who you don't know personally, but who has influenced you for the better.

One fascinating study showed that participants who wrote a letter of thanks once a week for eight weeks became significantly happier. The effects were even more powerful if they put a lot of effort into their letters.

Writing a letter of heartfelt thanks will affect your emotions even as you write it. And when you re-read it, hours or days later, it will have the same effect, filling you with appreciation, thankfulness and a sense of being connected to the person the letter is for.

Finding the Good in the Bad

It's hard, obviously, to be grateful for stuff that has happened to us which we feel furious about or wish had never happened. And yet I have learned that even in the worst of times there is always some good in the bad things – and I've come to believe that it's important to acknowledge them and to be grateful for them.

Someone might lose a job and it might seem like the end of the world. And yet a few months later that person could be re-employed and find, perhaps to their surprise, that the new job is much better and happier for them than the old one.

It's very common, too, for us to be at our lowest ebb when a relationship ends and to believe that nothing nice will ever happen again – and certainly to be convinced that we will never find love again. And yet we do.

It is my belief that we should allow ourselves to be grateful for good parts of bad experiences. I think it makes us better people and encourages our minds to get rid of any bitterness.

Should we go further and as well as acknowledging our gratitude actually say 'thank you' to someone who may once have hurt us? This is a tough one. Personally I feel that often just accepting and feeling some gratitude in these circumstances is all we need to do. But I do know people who have written to their ex-partners – usually some while after the break-up – and who have thanked those partners for the good times that preceded the split. I can think of one woman in particular. She wrote a letter to her former husband expressing sorrow that they had both hurt each other a great deal during the divorce, and she also thanked him for the love and companionship they had once shared and for giving her their two children. She told me that she felt better just for having written it, but that the big bonus was that her ex wrote a similar letter back to her and as a result they both now found they could co-parent their children in a much more friendly and co-operative way.

So maybe this is something to think about. You may have a new life now and renewed confidence but you may decide that you can draw a line better under something that once hurt you by showing gratitude for the bits of it that were good. This isn't for everyone. But it might be a useful strategy for you.

Lin Woolmington, whom I got to know when she came along to the Foundation and whom took part in our Ideal Home Show Diversity Catwalk, is someone who has proved that gratitude is possible even in the toughest of circumstances. Lin went through a harrowing ordeal, and yet she is one of the brightest, most cheerful and grateful people I have ever met. I'll let Lin tell you her extraordinary story.

Unexpected Joy – Lin's Story

A few years back I was suffering from severe depression. I don't know where it came from, because I had a good life. At 62 I had a happy marriage to my husband Colin, we'd been together since I was 17, we had paid off our mortgage and I had retired from my part-time secretarial job. Our daughter had long since grown up and left home and I found myself with time on my hands. But instead of doing all the things I'd planned and looked forward to for retirement, I sank into a deep clinical depression. Suddenly all the joy in life disappeared, I found no pleasure in anything and my confidence drained away.

I have absolutely no memory of the day of my accident but it seems I walked into town to do some shopping. The only thing I bought was a train ticket from our local station in Godalming, Surrey, but I never caught a train. Instead I was airlifted from the live railway track to the Royal London Hospital.

I sustained life-threatening high-voltage electrical burns and I owe my miraculous survival to the incredible skills and care of the Kent, Surrey and Sussex Air Ambulance and the hospital trauma medical team. I have no idea whether I fell or jumped and I decided not to see the CCTV footage because I didn't want to risk haunting flashbacks.

When I woke up Colin was on one side of me and a nurse was on the other. She was holding a pair of tweezers and leeches were plopping into her lap. She'd been using them to clean one of my wounds.

Colin had to tell me that I had lost my left arm and had a major head injury that had severely damaged the right side of my head, including my right eye and ear. Skin from my thighs had been grafted onto my head and my right little finger had been grafted back onto my hand.

My reaction to all of this was not distress or shock. What I felt, to the very core of my being, was happy to be alive. My depression had vanished, I felt very comfortable and nothing hurt. My confidence was back and, despite my injuries, I felt I could do or take on anything. I was in hospital for five months and during that time Dr Zane Perkins, who had been on the air ambulance, came to see me. I had asked to meet him to thank him, I was so very grateful because without the air ambulance and the prompt actions of that doctor and the pilot and medic on board, I wouldn't have made it.

I came out of hospital with a prosthetic arm and a whole new lease of life. Subsequently, after many reconstructive operations, I eventually also had a prosthetic eye and ear. In those first weeks back home my new arm took some getting used to – I fell over a few times and when I'm at home I still prefer not to wear it, though I did get the hang of wearing it to go out.

It was my plastic surgeon, Professor Myers, who told me about the Katie Piper Foundation. I'd been left partially bald because of the burns on my head and it was through the Foundation that I was given a new head of hair using the brilliant hair-weave system called Intralace – a nine-hour procedure that meant I could throw away my wigs. That was wonderful and certainly one of the best things to happen to me. I also attended workshops and met a lot of other burns survivors, who became friends.

The more you talk to someone the less you see their scars, you see the person.

In the years since the accident I have never stopped being grateful that I'm alive. I appreciate and give thanks for every detail of my life now. If I hadn't made it I wouldn't have known the amazing joy of being a grandmother. And my life today is so busy that I wonder how I ever found time to work. I give talks on behalf of the Foundation; it's a pleasure to stand up and tell my story to an audience. I also do all kinds of other things – from singing in a gospel choir to swimming, walking, playing Scrabble and keep fit. I'm over 70 now, but I feel great. Colin and I laugh a lot together and after more than 50 years together, we enjoy life.

Whenever I think about my life now, I get a feeling inside that I call my 'soda fountain' effect. It fills me with joy and elation. I fizz with joy, gratitude and confidence. I know now that I have the power to control my life. If there's something I don't like or don't want to do, I have the confidence to say so.

It's impossible for me to explain why, but ever since the accident I've been the same old Lin I was before the depression – and then some. I'm more confident and outgoing than I ever was before. Now there are no 'buts' in my life, I just do it. Perhaps because I've understood that the life I almost lost is so very precious.

When We Need Gratitude

It's great always to be appreciative, but there are times in life when it's more important than ever to be grateful.

We need gratitude the most when we:

- Feel stuck in life
- Can't see the point of going on
- Doubt ourselves
- Feel heartbroken over a lost relationship or the death of someone we care for
- Worry about someone close to us, like a troubled teenager.

At times like these it's hard to see the positive. And that's where gratitude can help. Put everything else on hold, don't try to fix or sort out yourself or anyone else, just spend a little time writing down all the things you have to be grateful for. We come to appreciate all the things that are not stuck in our lives that are worth carrying on for, that we can value about the people around us. Gratitude helps us see our situation in a way that can calm panic, and could open up our thinking to new solutions. When you can see the good as well as the bad in a situation, it becomes more difficult to stay stuck.

So recognise what you are grateful for, acknowledge it and appreciate it, and you may just find that you have a different perspective on the challenges you face.

Gratitude changes lives; it's as simple and as amazing as that.

CHAPTER 15

Connection

We all long for a deep, meaningful and lasting connection with someone we truly love, and who loves us. It's something so special and precious that when you find it you feel as though you've just won the crown jewels. And yet a relationship like that can be so hard to find, and sometimes we can come close – only to blow it by pushing the other person away, or refusing to let them get close, leaving us miserable and heartbroken.

Believe me, I've been through these scenarios and more. And what I've learned is that when you are authentic, when you accept who you are, with all your limitations and all your possibilities, when you know you are vulnerable but you reach out anyway, when you aren't afraid to be real, then you find the depth of connection that goes with true confidence.

The thing is, we are all vulnerable, and most of us try to hide it. But people with self-esteem and deep inner confidence aren't afraid to let their vulnerability show.

What we don't realise is that what makes you vulnerable also makes you beautiful. We're not invincible, but we try to appear that way. We put on a tough shell and then refuse to let anyone in. I know because that's what I did. When I first fell in love with Richie I pushed him away, sure he would leave anyway, until I realised one day that I'd found a wonderful man who wanted to be with me and who loved me just as I am. And if I didn't let him in, he was going to leave. I learned so much through that time; it wasn't easy letting someone get close to me, especially after I'd been through a couple of horrible rejections, but it was worth it. So don't be afraid to let someone come close, or to be the one to say I love you. Let yourself be seen for who you really are, because connection with others is what truly matters most in life.

In the pages that follow I'll tell you a bit about my own story of finding love – and I'll share some wonderful strategies and tips for letting love into your life.

Of course, we all have many connections in our lives, and our romantic connection with a partner is just one. The connections we make with family, friends and those we work with are also so vital to our happiness. The ability to get to know someone, and let them get to know you, and to be able to resolve issues and conflicts between you, is so important. We need the backing of strong, open and honest relationships if we're to be truly confident. And we need to have confidence in our relationship skills.

Meeting Richie

I was introduced to Richie by a good friend who told me Richie had seen my picture and said he'd like to get to know me.

It wasn't long after I'd dipped my toe into the dating pool again and been badly bitten, so I was very wary – I'd been left sitting in a restaurant by a guy who walked out on me, so my dating confidence was pretty low. For a while I thought I just wouldn't try again, ever. I had a savings account I'd started in the hope of adopting a child and I'd decided I was going to be married to my work and leave adult relationships to one side.

So when my friend told me about Richie, it threw me. But eventually I agreed, very cautiously, that he could get in touch. He sent me a text, I sent him one back, and after a bit of swapping messages we talked on the phone. He sounded so nice – relaxed, funny and easy-going. He told me we'd been in the same bars and that he'd seen me around, although I didn't remember seeing him. I really liked him on the phone so something in me thought, 'OK, I'll make this the last one.' But then again, I had thought the previous guy was going to be the last one.

We agreed to meet for a drink and to go to see a film and he offered to make the two-hour journey from his home in East London to West London, where I lived.

I told myself I had nothing to lose and it didn't matter if things went wrong, but of course I was still really nervous and wanted him to like me. I had bought a new outfit but I tried it on and it felt all wrong, so I chucked it on the floor and then tried about four more outfits before I found something I felt good in.

As I was about to leave he rang and said he was stuck in traffic and was going to be late. It was only ten minutes for me to get to the place where we'd agreed to meet, so I waited at home. In that pause I looked in the mirror and decided I looked awful so I changed again – and ended up being late.

Once I'd apologised we went for a drink – soft, as we were both driving – and we got on really well. He was great looking and good company. But we were only just starting to get to know one another so I was a bit tense during the film, because it felt quite strange to be sitting so close to someone I didn't really know yet.

Afterwards he needed to head straight off, as he had a long drive back and work in the morning. We both went to my car so that I could drive him to where his was, and as we said goodnight there was a toe-curling moment when he leaned towards me and I panicked. What was the etiquette now? I hadn't been in that situation for five years, so I leaned in a bit awkwardly for a kiss and at that moment he turned his head and I ended up licking his cheek. It was terrible! As I drove off, my cheeks burning, I was sure I had blown it and would never see him again.

Two days later he sent me a text, 'Hi, how are you?' He'd probably just been waiting so that he didn't seem too in-your-face, but that two-day wait had been agonising for me, so when his text arrived I was ready to bring out the brass band! Although I still wasn't at all sure where it was all going.

After that we talked on the phone and texted a lot. It was hard to meet because we were two hours apart and we were both busy. I was glad that he had his own life, friends and career and when we did manage to meet up again we had lots to talk about.

When I first met him I had let him see the work Katie Piper – bright, bubbly and confident – so I was conscious that this was who he liked. I hadn't got to the point of trusting him enough that I could let the barriers down and let him meet the other Katie – the one who's not always 'up', who gets fed up with hospitals and tired at the end of a working day.

Then my surgeons told me they were going to perform surgery on my nose. It was a major procedure in which they would be taking cartilage from my rib and a graft from my head to construct a new nose.

I had to break it to Richie. At that stage we had been dating for a little while, but it hadn't got to the committed couple stage. He was a young, single, good-looking guy and surgery like that places a lot of strain on a new relationship. I didn't want him to feel under pressure so I told him we should stop seeing each other for a bit and perhaps get back in touch in a few months' time.

Richie looked hurt. 'Why?' he asked.

I tried to explain that I wouldn't think it shallow of him to want an out at that stage, but he insisted he had no intention of backing out.

At the time I felt miserable that the surgery had to be done then, but now I think it was a good thing, because it brought us much closer. In the weeks while I was waiting to go in for the surgery Richie had started coming over to my little flat in the evenings and at weekends.

One evening he said, 'Let's go to the shops and get some food for an evening of telly' but I said, 'You go, I'll stay here.'

'Why?' Richie said. 'You haven't had the surgery yet, you're not ill.'

I explained that when I went out everybody stared and talked about me behind my back. But he just thought it was stupid and told me he wasn't worried. So we went to Sainsbury's and people did talk about me and he was fine, just completely relaxed about it.

Once I got to hospital he never flinched, even when I had an osmosis expander put into my nose. It's a small thing, the size of a grain of rice, and it was meant to gently stretch my nose, but it expanded too much, bursting through the burned skin, which had no stretch in it, and creating a hole in my face.

To make matters worse the hole became infected and it led to a blood infection. I felt terrible and I looked a wreck.

Richie would turn up at the hospital every night after work and just sit with me. He often came in his work clothes and he bought himself take-aways and just chatted to me. He hadn't met my family, but he got to know them there.

After the procedure, when I was allowed to go home, I couldn't walk because you can't put weight on the side of the body where the rib cartilage has been removed, so I was stuck in my upstairs flat, in bed or tottering along using walking sticks.

Talk about attractive. I had a hole in my side with a drain while I was in hospital, but at least that was removed when I was discharged. I also had to get up in the middle of the night to take medication and of course my new nose was still a swollen mass.

Once again I told Richie that he should get on with his life and stay in contact by phone. He just said, 'Are you kidding? You'll get so bored, this is perfect for me, I can sit with you and hang out here.'

Once I was up and about and I thought the worst was over, there was a hideous moment when the expanders shaping my new nose broke through, leaving an actual hole so that you could see into my nose and snot would drip through the hole. I'm used to dreadful things like that happening and everyone staring at me but I said to Richie that I didn't want to put him through the embarrassment of going out and about with me like that. He just said, 'Don't be ridiculous, I'm proud of you, I'm not embarrassed to go out with you.'

I think that was the point where I realised that nothing was going to put him off. If months of sleepless nights, drains, holes in my nose and bald patches hadn't sent him running, then I could grow old, saggy and overweight and he'd still be there.

In a way that experience weeded out so many of the questions I might have had at the beginning. Richie was by my side through it all, he saw grumpy Katie, ill Katie and bored Katie; there was no question any longer of putting on a show for him.

In those early days Richie had so much to deal with. I kept trying to push him away, and when he wouldn't go I got drunk and shouted at him. I just couldn't believe that anyone could love me. I used to say, 'You're going to break up with me anyway' and he'd say, 'No, I'm not.'

Richie always had natural confidence. He was, and is, steady and calm and resilient. So he dealt with whatever I threw at him incredibly well. But there did come a point where he told me I had to stop pushing him away because he was reaching his limit. I was drinking too much and picking fights with him. And I realised he was right. I knew that if I didn't I would lose him. It wasn't easy, but I did it, by giving up drinking for a while (I drink moderately now), and getting some counselling.

What We Bring Each Other

What helped me to stop pushing Richie away was the realisation that our relationship was not one-sided. He wasn't doing me a favour or feeling sorry for me; he loved me because I had a lot to give him, too.

We loved one another as a package, for everything we brought

243

to the relationship. Richie wasn't perfect, he could be a bit of a worrier, he could stick his head in the sand if he didn't want to talk about something and he was great at avoiding putting up the curtains when I asked him to! And I wasn't perfect either. Part of my package was the medical stuff, but it wasn't everything – it was only a part of it. I also brought knowledge and experience, capability and know-how, which Richie loved. Not many things daunt me now, and he admires that.

What he brought me was balance. I used to have a lot of highs and lows, but Richie is very consistent and some of that has rubbed off on me. I found a best friend in him, and that has been wonderful – we have a lot of fun together.

When you're with someone else you become less absorbed in your own problems. You think about the other person's needs, interests and experience and you learn to compromise and to share.

When I think of us I think about the great Marilyn Monroe quote: 'If someone doesn't love you at your worst they don't deserve you at your best.'

For our wedding vows Richie had to write down for the vicar the things he liked about me – as well as all the things he disliked. He said he knew that whatever happened to him I would always be there to help him, to problem solve and to pick up the pieces. And he liked the security of knowing that. So it doesn't matter that my nose isn't straight. If he met somebody who had a straight nose but didn't have my qualities then it wouldn't work for him. He is a realist; he is not going to pretend that I have a straight nose. But it doesn't matter because of what else I bring into his life. The good things about me make his life better, just as his qualities make mine better.

A couple of years back I needed to have small tubes inserted into my nose to keep it from collapsing. I have coped with looking different because that is permanent, but to have an apparatus there that is not part of me was a bit weird. I asked Richie how bad it was and he kept saying, it really doesn't matter, it is like a fashion thing. So I thought, oh good. Then the next day I was on a job and the film crew I was working with said, 'Oh my god, you've ruined the continuity of the show, how are we going to cut and edit, the tubes look really in-your-face.' I didn't mind their honesty, I like that they always treat me as perfectly normal, but I had to laugh, because Richie had convinced me the tubes were hardly noticeable and of course that wasn't true at all. I loved him for the fact that he just thought it was irrelevant. He doesn't care, he says to me, you're my type, and that's all there is to it.

After what happened to me I couldn't be a controlling or jealous person and Richie certainly isn't, we trust one another and that's at the core of everything. He wouldn't ever go through my emails or phone calls if I was away filming and having dinner at the hotel together with male colleagues. He wouldn't worry, he knows we are in love, we are sure of one another, and that makes us good partners.

Now that I'm in the public eye Richie leads a hard life with me because he is always ignored when we go to restaurants or events. He is the person people will turn their backs on, they come up to us and introduce themselves to me and don't even ask him his name or notice him, except to ask him to take a picture of them with me! But he is intelligent enough to know that I need to go out publicly to increase the profile of the charity and because I'm passionate about changing the taboo around how disfigured people are seen.

Be Realistic about Relationships

If you want to have a satisfying relationship you have to be realistic. There's no point looking for the perfect man or woman, because they don't exist. It's much better to see someone's faults and weaknesses and love them anyway.

Most happy relationships work because both people see who the other is and accept them. They don't want to change them or to set them up to be perfect. At the same time, they don't accept wrong or cruel treatment – there are some things that just aren't acceptable.

I often meet people who say things like,' Why do I always meet guys who hit me?' or 'What are the chances of meeting three women in a row who let me down?' The answer is – you need self-awareness. If you keep making the same mistake then you're not looking at the choices you make and why you make them.

On the other hand I meet people who say, 'My partner is wonderful but he's not perfect, he can be pretty self-absorbed and that's not always easy to live with, but the benefits of the relationship outweigh the drawbacks by a long way.'

Self-awareness means that instead of letting life, and relationships, 'just happen' you know that you are making choices and you put thought and effort into making choices that will work for you.

Self-awareness goes hand in hand with confidence. To be confident and happy in a relationship, you need to go into it with your eyes open.

Vulnerability

So often we avoid feeling vulnerable by numbing ourselves. And we do this in all kinds of ways – with drink, drugs, eating, spending and so on. We do these things to shut out feelings like fear and shame, to shut out painful memories and to avoid having to open ourselves to anyone, for fear of getting hurt.

The trouble is, you can't just numb one feeling, you numb them all. Which means you also numb joy, gratitude and happiness. If you want those wonderful feelings in your life, you must let in the painful ones, too, because that's how it works.

After the attack I was no stranger to feeling vulnerable. I felt vulnerable in all kinds of ways, physically and emotionally. The worst thing was losing my eyesight. When the acid was thrown in my face I was immediately blinded in both eyes and for a long time I didn't know if I would ever see again.

I did eventually get back the sight in one eye, but it was a long process. The other eye can still only make out light and shade and movement, no details at all.

Going through that made me understand that something as basic as sight can be lost in a few moments, and that makes you vulnerable. So I became tough, because it was the only way to cope. Except that being tough can cut you off; it's a defence mechanism and you can go too far and end up feeling very alone, shutting out people and feelings. I drank more than I should, because it helped to numb the pain. But it numbed joy, too, and that's why I stopped. Better to have all your feelings, including the vulnerable ones, than none.

When I won a Woman of the Year Award in 2011 I appeared onstage in front of hundreds of people to receive the award. It was an amazing moment, capping everything I had been through in the years since the attack. But that night I went back to my little flat on my own and just sat there with a drink. I had no one to share my achievement with. I could have called a friend, or my parents, but it was late and it didn't seem fair.

Meeting Richie, and learning to share my life with him, was scary, challenging and wonderful. And it gives me joy every day to know that now I am not alone, I am choosing to be open and honest about who I am, with someone who is doing the same.

Shame

One of the biggest reasons why people feel afraid to open up is shame. So many of us feel shame, for something that happened to us, something we did, something in our past, or sometimes we just carry it as a legacy. Shame can be a terribly destructive emotion, making us feel worthless and bad. I understand it well, because before the acid attack the man who organised the attack raped me and held me prisoner in a hotel room. And although I had been the one wronged, I felt guilty and ashamed for being fooled by him, and for allowing myself to get into that situation. I judged myself and was afraid that other people would judge me, too.

It took me some time to get past that all-encompassing sense of shame. But when I decided to make the documentary *My Beautiful Face* I gave up my right to anonymity as the victim of a sex crime. I was aware that everyone who saw the film would know who I was and what had happened, so I felt very vulnerable indeed. And I had no idea just how many people would see the film. But an amazing thing happened – as the film went public I received so much warmth and support, and suddenly I didn't feel ashamed any longer. I understood then, not just theoretically but really, deep down understood, that I was not in any way to blame. Opening up and telling people who I was and what had happened helped me.

It was a real lesson in the power of vulnerability, I'd been afraid that giving up my anonymity was a huge mistake, but in fact it was the opposite, it helped me to heal.

Researcher and storyteller Brené Brown, famous for her books and talks about vulnerability, has said that shame derives its power from being unspeakable. So to deprive it of power, speak about it. I know that isn't easy, but you don't have to tell the world, just tell someone you trust. Because shining a light on it begins to dissolve shame.

Don't let shame define you or dictate your choices and decisions. Shame can keep you stuck and closed down. Make the choice instead to let go of shame and take the first step, by talking about it to someone you trust.

Being Authentic

So what does it take to be fully authentic? In other words, to show the real you, the things you think of as good or bad, your vulnerabilities and your strengths, to someone you want to share your life with.

It's important, of course, that you trust the person you are going to open up to. That means getting to know them, being aware of who they are and whether they are worthy of your trust. I'm not suggesting you throw yourself wide open to just anyone, because that's the way to get needlessly hurt. Opening up is a process that happens between the two of you; some psychotherapists call it the dance of intimacy, because it works a little like a dance – you take a step forward and then they do, they take the next step and then you do. It's a process of mutual trust and respect that is about investing in the relationship and making it as strong as possible.

Here are the four pillars of authenticity:

1. Courage

You need all the courage you can get to show someone all of who you are. You have to be willing to take the risk that maybe the other person won't love or want all of you. But it's worth digging deep for your courage, to make the leap from fear of rejection to allowing for that possibility and doing it anyway.

2. Self-regard

What do I mean by self-regard? I mean valuing and respecting yourself. How can you expect someone else to value and respect you if you don't show yourself that kind of care and protection? And the good thing is that if the other person doesn't respond by valuing and respecting you, it doesn't matter so much, because you're doing it for yourself.

3. Practice

Showing your vulnerable side isn't something you do just once. We show our authentic selves a bit at a time. There are moments when you feel more guarded, and moments when you feel you can open up. But there are also times when you need to push yourself to open up, so that you get better at it. If someone you trust is inviting you to tell them about your innermost thoughts and feelings, take the opportunity.

4. Joy

When you do trust and open up, rather than feeling terrified that you've done the wrong thing, let yourself enjoy the flow of positive feelings that come with being who you are and showing that to someone else. The connection that happens when you trust and open up is very special. And while the intimacy of opening up to someone you love is wonderful, you can also begin to be more authentic with friends and family – and reap the benefits.

Visualisation – The Castle

This is a great visualisation for helping you to let down your defences and open up:

Sit comfortably, eyes closed, and imagine you are in a castle, surrounded by a wide moat. The drawbridge is up and you are invincible, well-armed and safe.

Now imagine slowly letting down the drawbridge. When it is fully down, see yourself venturing across it, out of the castle into the world outside. Imagine yourself exploring what lies outside – a green field, a road, a small town. When you've had enough, go back across the drawbridge into the castle and then pull up the drawbridge.

Understand that you can do this as often as you like – you are in control. You can stay in the castle, or you can put the drawbridge down and venture out, knowing that you can return and raise the drawbridge whenever you like.

Now open your eyes again.

The image of the castle and the drawbridge is really useful as a metaphor for opening up. And the important thing is that you realise you are in control of the process. You open up when you want to, for as long as you want to, and you can stop at any time.

Be Willing to Open Up

It is so liberating being with someone who knows all about you. Life is exciting; there's no more hiding things you think are unacceptable, or just showing off the glossy bits. Of course you need to make an effort, you can't spend the rest of your life in a pair of pyjamas, but you don't have to hide anything about yourself, and that's an amazing feeling.

I still struggle sometimes with what I feel are the undesirable aspects of me, although to Richie nothing about me is undesirable. So I understand how exposed someone can feel when opening up to a new partner. But if you don't open up then you don't allow for the possibility of real closeness.

I believe that to find your inner strength you have to face your vulnerability. It's easy to be so much of a coper that people think you don't need a relationship, you can do it all on your own and then you end up isolating yourself. It can be a good thing to show someone that you need them, that you can't do it all on your own and don't want to. Being willing to need someone else is not a weakness, it's a strength.

I didn't want to let myself depend on Richie because I was afraid I'd lose him. But once I realised that he was in this relationship for good, I let go and began to really trust him.

When we let go of needing to be in control and allow ourselves to be softer and more open, we grow in confidence and strengthen our connections with the people we love.

CHAPTER 16

What Story Will You Tell?

We all love to tell stories. We tell a friend a funny story about someone we met, we tell someone we meet at a party a story about our job or family and we go home and tell our families stories about the day we've had.

Telling stories is part of being human, it's one of the ways in which we connect with one another and it's a way of sharing information about who we are. So the stories we tell about our lives, and the way we tell them, are important.

Your life is a story, and you have to decide, at every turning point, what kind of a story it's going to be. It's easy to tell the story of something nice that's happened; a great piece of news, a win, a success or something that we enjoyed. But it can be harder to tell the story of something tough, painful or distressing. And we have to make choices about the way we tell the story, and how big a part of our whole life story we're going to let it be. Because the way we tell the stories, to ourselves and to others, influences the way we lead our lives and the future choices we make.

When something goes wrong we can give up and say that we let it change the course of our lives, or we can choose to look back and say it was just a small part of what happened. We can have a story about being derailed by an event or experience, or we can have a story that says we got past it and didn't let it dictate the future.

Sometimes I ask myself, 'Will you say I got out there and faced my fears and had a go, or will you say I went back to bed and gave up?' It's an important question, especially on the days when I feel like going back to bed – and believe me, there are some of those.

To be lived with confidence, life has to be lived with meaning. That means we have to do something that matters, something that is worthwhile and makes a difference. And that almost always involves courage and effort. For me, that begins with the story you tell yourself each day.

My Dating Story

Let me explain what I mean. One of the best examples I can give is about the time in my life when I started dating again. It was about three years after the attack, I'd moved out of my parents' house and into my own flat and I was working to build the Foundation. After years of operations to rebuild my face, while I knew all the medical procedures would still carry on, I felt ready to have a bit of a social life and I began to hope that I might meet a man – the kind of lovely, intelligent man who would look past the scars to who I was.

It was terrifying putting myself out there again. I did my hair –

always my calling card – and make-up and went out a few times with my good friend Kay. Guys would come over to us to chat her up and I would get the mates, who would either ask me endless questions about the attack or ignore me and play on their phones. It was humiliating and a painful contrast to how things had been before the attack, when I took for granted being pretty and guys being interested in me.

One evening Kay and I went to a new bar. The lighting was low and the atmosphere was buzzy, and a guy came over and started chatting to me. He seemed nice and he asked for my number. When he sent me a text the next day I was really excited. We chatted about this and that until he asked what my job was. I told him I worked for a small charity that he probably wouldn't have heard of, the Katie Piper Foundation. He sent a text back, 'Oh my God, have you ever met her?'

I wasn't sure what to think. I'd introduced myself as Kate, so maybe he genuinely didn't realise. I sent him a text, 'Ha ha. Yeah, because I am Katie Piper xx'.

He never replied. Just like that I was rejected. And it hurt. I thought about it for days, wondering how someone could just cut you off like that.

I wasn't sure I wanted to try again, but a few weeks later Kay and some other friends persuaded me to go on a girls' night out. There were five of us, and as luck would have it, we met a group of five guys and ended up hanging out and dancing with them into the small hours.

One of the guys seemed really nice, and he pulled me aside and asked me if I wanted to go out with him. I panicked. The place we were in wasn't well-lit – did he know I was burned?

I agreed to go out with him and he mentioned a very smart restaurant and said he'd book a table. That made me feel even more nervous, I'd have preferred a relaxed pub.

On the evening of our date we agreed to meet outside, and I was painfully aware that the setting sun was in my face, showing up every detail. And as soon as we met I could see that he was shocked. He stared, his mouth open, and didn't say a word.

I did my best to be bright and breezy as we went in and were seated. I chatted away, trying to keep the conversation going, but I could tell that he just wanted a way out. And then he found it – before we'd even ordered he said he'd spotted some work colleagues and was going to pop over and say hi. He shot off, desperate to get away, while I was left sitting at the table alone, sipping my diet coke.

Half an hour later my worst fears were confirmed. As I peered around the restaurant there was no sign of him – he clearly wasn't coming back. Trying not to cry, I had to get up, walk across the restaurant, retrieve my coat and leave, clinging to the last shreds of my dignity, under the curious gaze of the staff and the other diners. Once I'd got into my car I cried until there were no tears left. I felt I'd set myself up to be hurt, and for a little while I thought, 'That's it, I'm not trying again.'

I knew I wanted children, and thinking that I was unlikely to get into a relationship that would allow that to happen, I set up a savings fund in the hope that I might have the chance to adopt or foster a baby. And while I nursed my bruised heart, I got on with work, which was keeping me increasingly busy. But as time went by and I thought about what happened I realised what I was doing. By refusing to ever try dating again I was allowing those thoughtless and unkind guys to dictate my future.

I had a choice – I could feel hopeless, never try to date again and spend my life alone, or I could decide that a couple of rejections don't make the whole story, get back out there and try again. After all, so what if those guys didn't like me? I was never going to see them again, so why should I let them matter?

What story was I going to tell?

Was I going to stay at home crying about someone who was not my destiny, while they had no doubt moved on and were dating someone else? No way! But if I wanted a different outcome to the story then I was going to have to make a different choice.

The story I wanted to tell was about moving on, past a couple of unimportant blips, and meeting the man I would be happy with and who would love and appreciate me.

I could have settled for the story that said, 'Well, I never married because I couldn't take any more rejection' or I could go for the one that would say, 'It took a while, but then I met the right man and I married him.'

And guess what, readers? That's what I did.

To make your story the one that you want, you have to be willing to take risks. I had to risk going on a date again, even though it was a very scary prospect.

It was easy to play the victim and think that the dates who stood me up didn't fancy me because I was burned – but the truth is they might not have fancied me because I'm blond or short or boring. It is easy to go to your biggest insecurity and to think that's responsible for everything that goes wrong, but even the most attractive person can get stood up. It's better just to think,

'Well, for whatever reason they didn't fancy me. That can happen to anyone, I'm not going to spend the rest of my twenties crying about it.'

So when, a few months later, my friend told me that Richie had asked for my number after seeing my photo, I had to decide whether I would risk it. I knew the photo didn't show much detail and I wondered whether I should warn him that I was burned. But why would I do that? You wouldn't warn someone you were about to date that you had cellulite or bad breath or big feet, so why would I tell him that I have skin grafts on my face and back? Instead I decided to do what anyone would do – play up my best points, like my hair, which always makes me feel more confident. And this time it was different. This time I met a man who, to my amazement, never saw my scars, he just saw me, he liked me and I liked him and we had a great date, that led to another and another . . .

Tell it in Different Ways

Here's a lovely exercise that shows just how easy it is to interpret anything that happens to us in different ways.

Think of a simple journey you made recently. It might be your journey to work, to the supermarket, to a friend's house or to a class or activity.

Now describe that journey, out loud:

- As a comedy – make it as funny as you can, imagine you're a comedian like Michael McIntyre, who manages to make the mundane and everyday seem hilarious.
- As a drama – add as much dramatic impact as you can.

Imagine it's a play, full of highs and lows, being described by a Shakespearean actor.

- As a tragedy – make the story as sad and heartbreaking as you can.
- As a disaster – this time you want it to be a bit like a disaster movie, full of suspense and major events.
- As a romance – this one might be a challenge, but imagine it's a story with Leonardo DiCaprio in it, or Jennifer Lawrence, and make it sexy and sultry.
- As a triumph – tell the story with a lot of excitement, building to a crescendo when you actually arrive!

It's a fun exercise and it's amazing how the same story sounds completely different each time, doesn't it? And yet it's the same journey. It's simply that you can choose to tell it in so many different ways. That's what I mean by choosing what story you are going to tell – that journey you described is no different to your life.

When You Get the Short Straw

There's no life without hurt, pain, trauma, upset, loss and bereavement. And, sometimes, some people seem to be tested beyond endurance, beyond what seems fair. If that's you, it's hard not to feel sorry for yourself. Why should you get the short straw in life?

There's no answer to that. Mostly we don't have a choice about what happens to us. We're not being punished for something, we didn't deserve it – we were just in that place at that time and something bad happened. What's more, we can't guarantee that other bad things won't happen. I once saw a counsellor who said to me, 'A bad thing happened to you, and other bad things may happen in the future. Having one really awful thing doesn't mean that you've somehow had your share. But you've coped, and you can deal with new difficulties if they come your way'. I was shocked at the time, but then I realised she was right. I had acid thrown in my face, and then a few years later my mum got cancer. It didn't seem fair at all, she had been so wonderful through everything that happened to me, and then she got sick. Thankfully she's doing well, but it's been a wobbly ride and there were moments when I felt our family had had more than our share of misery. But that's life, stuff happens and you have to deal with it. And I coped with it, I had found my inner strength and it was there when a fresh challenge came along.

And that's the point. Because we can choose how we deal with it. The way you react can be the making of you – an opportunity to find your strength, courage and resilience. An opportunity to decide how your story will go – whether it will be full of self-pity and doubt, or whether it will be the kind of story that inspires other people.

Sometimes you don't know how well you can cope until you are tested. When things get difficult you can find your strength emerges. You discover how big you are.

When something tough happens, decide whether it's going to be 10 per cent of your story, or 90 per cent. Are you going to let it define you, or are you going to move beyond it?

You have to be tough and stubborn to move on. I was angry after what happened to me, but I channelled the anger into a force for good. I felt defiant – why should I let the bad guys win?

Sometimes we think life is so complicated, but in fact it's simple – you either do something or you don't. You only ever have two choices.

Make Your Story Happen

I believe that you decide what you want in life, and then you go out and make it happen. No one thought disabled people could be supreme athletes until we saw the Paralympians and were in awe of them. In the London 2012 Olympics they were extraordinary – gifted, dedicated, brilliant. We all fell in love with them and they turned around attitudes towards those with disabilities.

I wanted to do the same thing – I wanted to turn around the widely held belief that someone with burns couldn't be sexy or beautiful or wear a gorgeous dress or present a programme on television.

Breaking down taboos is one of my goals, and I know there are other people who feel the same way. Who writes the rules? We do!

I was never going to give my attackers the satisfaction of being the girl whose life they ruined. I never want to give them that end to the story. Instead I choose what I want to be and then I go out there and do everything I can to be it.

You can, too. Success is a journey, not a destination. It doesn't happen in a straight line, the path goes off to one side and then the other all the time. But when it veers off track you just get back on it and keep going. Create your own future, and your own closure. Don't look for happiness in other people, find it in yourself.

When I married in November 2015 I remember thinking that it had been a long journey. It had been almost eight years since the attack that nearly killed me, and there I was, marrying the most wonderful man. I'd had health problems and we'd already put the wedding off once, and I thought we might have to put it off again. But we didn't and it all went to plan – despite my anxious checking and re-checking! Richie and I were both emotional, in fact I think just about everyone was in tears. And I had never been more sure of anything, or happier.

Raiche's Story

Raiche Mederick is a remarkable example of a woman who, in the face of enormous odds, has chosen to tell a story of triumph over adversity, achievement and generosity to others.

Raiche, now in her twenties, was just 18 months old when she was burned in a house fire. She had 70 per cent burns on her face and body and she was on life-support for months. The toes on her left foot and the tips of the fingers of her right hand had to be amputated and the accident left her facially disfigured and with permanent scars on much of her body. Because she was so young there was very little unburned skin that doctors could use for grafts and, as the grafted skin didn't grow with her, she needed numerous operations and she will be having them for the rest of her life.

Raiche has had to put up with stares, comments and thoughtless cruelty all her life – not to mention a great deal of pain. She could be forgiven for feeling sorry for herself, but that's not Raiche. She is outgoing, funny, talkative and great company. Naturally happy, she has a positive effect on everyone around her.

Determined and hard-working, Raiche studied tour management at a CATO music academy and has a passion for charity and events. So much so that she plans to start a charity for adult burns survivors.

Raiche took part in our Diversity Catwalk at the Ideal Home Show in 2015 and she looked amazing, first in a smart business suit and then in a sexy black swimming costume. She often comes along to Foundation events and she's wonderful with those who are feeling less confident.

Raiche has never sat around feeling sorry for herself. She has energy and vitality and she's one of life's givers. Hers is the story of a winner, someone who is making a positive difference in the world.

So what was it that helped Raiche to turn her tragedy into such a fantastic story?

'I was very shy when I was small,' she laughs. 'But what helped me was my mum, who always taught me to hold my head up high and be proud of who I was, and the Children's Burns Club. My brother was also burned in the fire and the club was started for us by a wonderful woman called Pat Wade, MBE. She was a play specialist who worked at the Billericay Burns Unit where I was treated and she realised that there was nothing out there to help children like me and my brother. She modelled the club on one she saw in the States and it gave us a childhood full of life-changing experiences, surrounded by other burned children just like us.

'Our mum was a single parent and didn't have the spare cash for holidays. But through the club we visited amazing destinations like Disneyland and Lapland. We lived for that week away every summer. We had water activities, kayaking, rock climbing, go-karting, aviation lessons, all kinds of adventures. Volunteers, many of them from the fire service, the ambulance service and the medical profession, came to support us and they helped us to push the boundaries of what we could do and to challenge ourselves both physically and mentally in a social environment.

'We also had Christmas parties, jamborees, summer barbecues, it's a knockout – all kinds of things that gave us a great time. It was a place where I could be totally free to be truly myself.

'All the kids had been burned, so no one stared or asked questions, unlike at school, where I had a hard time. The club was like a family, and Pat, who got the MBE for all she did, was like our grandmother. Because of what she did I found my confidence and self-belief.'

When Raiche turned 18 she had to leave the club, which was only for children aged seven to 17. She returned as a volunteer and fundraiser, and she began to think about starting a club for adult burns survivors.

Then, in 2012, Raiche watched *My Beautiful Face* and she got in touch with the Katie Piper Foundation. She came along to some of our workshops and in 2014 she had a hair replacement system and eyebrow tattoos.

'That was amazing,' Raiche grins. 'The burns had left me with hair loss, and although I'd worn wigs they could be hot and itchy. The weave, of human hair, was beautifully done and with that and the eyebrows I felt so feminine.

'The Foundation has taught me all kinds of things, including how to prepare for interviews, and opened my eyes to life as an adult burns survivor. That gave me the courage to live independently in the summer of 2015 and now I'm making plans for my own charity.

'Taking part in the diversity catwalk show was such a good

experience. I met other wonderful women and it gave me the courage to wear gorgeous clothes outside my comfort zone. The stylist encouraged me to show off my shoulders and to wear a swimsuit and the audience's warm reception helped calm my nerves.

'My life isn't always easy. I still get people staring and reacting unpredictably. They sometimes seem afraid of my scars, instead of just asking me for the story behind them. I don't mind talking about it – I was a baby, and it was just something that happened.

'Still, I don't have time to be down – my mates don't allow it. I have an amazing group of friends. Our bonds are so special, and we live in each other's homes. They give me so much support.

'I always wanted my story to be about what I'd achieved despite what happened, not a sob story about poor me. I don't know what the future holds, but I'm excited. It's going to be an interesting road. I have all kinds of plans and hopes and I'm going to do my best to make them all happen.'

Raiche, and others like her, fill me with hope and make me so glad that the Foundation exists and is able to bring so many good people together. Every day I see people who have been through tough ordeals make the decision not to let what's happened define the rest of their lives. And once that decision is made, they begin to think about the story they really want to be able to tell.

Be Adaptable

Things are always changing. The best-laid plans can go wrong. So we need to be adaptable and to learn to cope when things go pear-shaped. We need to be able to tell the story of how we saved the day, found a way round or had a good time anyway, not how everything went wrong and it all got spoiled.

I've had to get more used to the fact that things are always changing than most people. I realised early on that I'd just have to work round the changes, or I'd be constantly frustrated.

I was so excited about Belle's first birthday – I'd been planning a big party for ages, I couldn't wait to spoil her and share all the fun with family and friends. I had to go into hospital shortly beforehand for a procedure to help me swallow, but I was assured I'd be home well before the big day. Except I wasn't. There were complications and I ended up in hospital with a tear in my oesophagus leading to surgical emphysema. There was no way I could come home, so Richie had to bring Belle to see me and all our plans for the big day were shelved.

I don't think Belle minded – she was only one, after all. But I minded; I wanted to share my daughter's first birthday with her. But I had to let it go, be adaptable and enjoy being with her for a short while.

When I came out of hospital I couldn't eat solid food for most of the year. I had to drink high-protein shakes. We had our wedding booked, we'd already moved it once, and I was thinking, 'I'm getting married and I can't even eat a piece of my own wedding cake!' It was sad, but it wasn't the end of the world. At least I made it to my wedding – a few months earlier when I'd been very ill I hadn't been sure I'd be able to do that. And it was a wonderful wedding; I wore a gorgeous dress, I could walk and talk and make a speech and have a drink and a bowl of soup. And I'll always be able to tell the story of the beautiful wedding I had and how special it was.

Life Choices

Life is a series of choices. We all make the wrong ones sometimes and we live with the consequences of those. But I think there are ways that you can help yourself make the right choice.

When it comes to most choices, there are a few simple rules that help:

Will your choice hurt anyone, including you?
Will your choice benefit anyone, including you?
Will you look back and be glad that you made this choice?
Is your choice going to make you happy?

In the early days with Richie, when I used to push him away, I was sure he'd leave me, so I thought I might as well speed up the process and get it over with – push him until he jumped. But then I realised how much I would regret that. The alternative was to stop pushing him away and begin to trust that he really did want to be with me.

I could choose to be alone (answers to the above questions would then be yes, no, no, no) or I could choose to be with this lovely man and have a life with him (answers to the above questions no, yes, yes, yes). When I looked at it that way, I knew it was a choice I had to make.

So when it comes to making choices, don't let anything stop you making the ones that will carry you forward, towards a better future. If you want to be happy, choose to do the things that will make you happy. Sometimes it takes courage to go for what you want, but if you don't you might always regret it. And only you can decide what story you are going to tell.

The Secret

I feel I've discovered something wonderful. I've cracked a secret that I just have to share. I will never get rid of my scars, never stop needing treatment. But I have found a way to live with them, and to live a truly good life, a worthwhile life, a life worth living. That, to me, is a miracle and I want to shout it from the rooftops and share it with everyone. No one can take that away from me – I have found a way to feel good about myself, to feel sexy and beautiful and happy when society says I shouldn't be. I feel passionately about this; it's something I want for others, too.

Every week I meet people who are at the start of the journey that I have been through. They've been burned and scarred and when they're just coming out of hospital they feel that life is as good as over. But I know that ten years from now they will feel differently. They can choose to tell a story of a new life, an exceptional life that dealt with the difficulties and the pain and the injuries and still achieved so much. I want them to blossom, because I know that they can.

I remember being a patient and thinking. 'Is my life over?' But it wasn't over; it was just a new stage of life beginning.

I remember being in the burns unit, soon after I came out of the coma, and hearing someone say to my parents, 'She probably won't be able to work again, at best she will live at home with you, dependent on you.' And I thought to myself, 'No way is that going to be the rest of my life, no way at all.'

The people who chose to attack me wanted it to be the biggest and worst thing to ever happen in my life, so I wanted it to be the opposite. I'm an energetic person, and I could have chosen to put all that energy into being angry and bitter, letting everyone know that my life was unfair. I could have stayed on disability benefits, refused to work, sat in a puddle of misery feeling sorry for myself. But that was never the story I wanted to tell.

So whatever has happened in your life so far – choose what story you want to tell. Make it a story of happiness, success, achievement, excitement, joy, love, friendship and fulfilment. Why would you settle for anything less?

CHAPTER 17

All-Round Confidence

I hope by now that you've been able to take some giant steps forward in your confidence journey. My goal is better confidence for all of us, in all the varied areas of our lives. I want every woman and man to feel that they can walk into any situation, head held high, and handle it with confidence and a sense of calm. We deserve nothing less.

It's funny how we can feel so much more confident in some areas than in others. Personally I feel the most confident when I'm at work. I can get up and talk in front of an audience, or lead a meeting and it doesn't worry me at all. And I feel confident as a mum; even though I'm still fairly new to it, I'm learning fast, on the job. But I feel out of my depth in a nightclub, I can't stand the noise and the crowds. A friend of mine said she'd be horrified by the idea of public speaking, but she feels really confident when she's the life and soul of a party.

Very few people feel the kind of inner confidence that means whatever the situation they can approach it with cool, calm self-belief. But this is what I hope and believe we can all have. Once we understand what confidence is really about and cultivate the belief that we really are OK, all of the time, in any situation, then anything becomes possible.

We may never feel equally confident in every area of our lives – there will always be some things that feel more challenging than others. But we can be confident enough to face anything, and we can keep on working to raise our confidence levels.

Feeling confident is so amazing – it makes you feel you can do anything, and that's exciting. It's the soda-fountain feeling that Lin Woolmington described when she spoke about being grateful to be alive. What wonderful possibilities we open up for ourselves when we step out in the morning feeling glad to be alive, happy and confident.

I've learned so much about confidence from other people. I've learned the cool, calm, grounded kind of confidence from Richie, the 'wow, everything is new and exciting' confidence from Belle, the courageous, face-the-music kind of confidence from my mum and the 'get-back-up-no-matter-what' kind of confidence from the brilliant women who took part in the Ideal Home Show Diversity Catwalk. Each of them has faced enormous challenges, and they've all found their own way through and, despite heartbreak and setbacks, they've come out stronger and more confident than ever.

One of the things I love most about life is learning from other people. Making connections, growing friendships and strong working relationships is the fabric of life. Everyone who comes into my life has something to teach me – even those who are negative help me find a way to be stronger.

When I give motivational talks I describe the attack very briefly because it's just the seed of what I want to say. Most of the 45 minutes or so that I'm talking is about how I took control and turned it around. One of my favourite sayings is that life is 10 per cent what happens to you and 90 per cent what you do with it afterwards. That's why the story I tell is not a horrendous one, it's a story of hope, it's about how I was able to move forward and have a good life in spite of what happened. And every time I tell the story of my recovery, the choices I faced and the life I made for myself, it makes me feel happy, because I am able to tell a story about turning something terrible that happened into something good.

Make sure that your story is a positive one, too. And remember that you are not alone. We are all in it together, all finding our way, and we can help and support one another.

Remember you have CONFIDENCE

I like to think of this book as a kind of confidence toolkit. Something you can dip into when you need a boost, a bit of friendly back up or a reminder of just how capable and amazing you are.

When you need it most, I want you to have confidence at your fingertips, as a reminder of all you are and all you can do. So here is my own guide to what confidence is about, for you, for me and for all of us.

Spelling our Confidence:

C – Choice
O – Optimism
N – Nurture
F – Feelings
I – Inner Resources
D – Dream
E – Esteem
N – No
C – Contribution
E – Energy

Choice

No matter what the situation, you always have a choice. We make hundreds of choices every day, even though we're not conscious of all of them. So think about your choices, and make them wisely. Let them always be for your good and the good of others.

If you are stuck, unhappy or repeating mistakes and bad choices, remember that life will change for you when you do something different. If you keep doing the same things, you will always get the same outcomes.

Sometimes the decision to do it differently can begin with something small. But the important thing is knowing that we do have a choice. We can choose the attitude we take to every day, and everything that happens in that day. While we can't change the past or other people, we can change what we do. We can turn a difficult situation into an easier one, we can be generous and we can help others.

Optimism

Don't look at how far up the mountain you have to climb. Instead think about how wonderful the view from the top will be. In other words, life is so much easier, things work so much better when you decide to be an optimist and not a pessimist. We can all find ourselves looking at what could go wrong. But it's a miserable way to live. Instead, focus on what could go right. And while you're waiting to see if it works out or not, you might as well feel good, rather than feeling bad.

It's been shown over and over again to be true that what we focus on grows. In other words, focus on the thing you dread and it's more likely to happen. Focus on the best possible outcome and you may well achieve it.

Being an optimist feels better, and it's good for you – the result of dozens of scientific studies has shown that the evidence connecting an upbeat outlook to a healthier life is incredibly strong. You really will live longer if you look on the bright side.

Nurture

Care for yourself, because no one else is with you 24 hours of every day of your life, so no one else can do it for you.

When we look after ourselves we're in a better position to look after others. On planes, in the safety briefing during take-off, the flight attendant tells the passengers that in the event of an accident adults should put on their own oxygen masks before putting them on babies and children. That's because if the adult can breathe, they will be in a better position to care for a child. It's a useful thing to remember – look after yourself not because you're selfish but because it's vital if you are to function well and do all of the other things you need and want to do. Most of us have responsibilities towards others – partners, children, elderly relatives, but if we wear ourselves out we're no good to them. So get enough sleep, eat well, exercise, have some time alone, pace yourself and don't forget to breathe deeply.

Feelings

There are a few really useful things to remember about feelings. We all have them, all the time, they are part of us. We can't help what we feel, but we can choose how to respond to those feelings. You can feel angry, but you don't need to act out, you can control it. You can feel unhappy, but you don't need to let it take you over. Why? Because the secret about feelings is this – feelings follow behaviour. This means that if you behave as if you are happy, you will start to feel happy, but if you behave as if you are sad, you will start to feel sad. So the important thing to watch is the way you behave. Act the way you would like to feel and you will feel that way. Our body language and physical selves have enormous power over our internal world. This means that you can behave as if you are confident – and then you will begin to feel more confident.

Inner Resources

We each have a well of powerful inner resources. Sometimes they get buried under layers of stuff – analysing, worrying and so on. But dig deep and you will find the resources that tell you what is best for you and can carry you through anything. So trust yourself to act in your own best interests. You are the one person you can absolutely count on, no matter what happens. Be consistently supportive and kind to yourself and stick with what you believe to be right. When you trust yourself you are not dependent on anyone else's opinion. You may ask for it and take it into account, but you won't act on it unless it fits with what you believe. Trust yourself to know what you need to do.

To build self-trust, keep the promises you make to yourself, speak kindly and positively to yourself, have faith in yourself and don't spend too much time with people who undermine you. With self-trust you build self-confidence, because they are two sides of the same coin.

Dream

Our dreams matter. Whether we are in the process of making them come true or they are on the distant horizon, dreams motivate us, encourage us and give us hope. We need something to work towards, whether it's a special holiday, an amazing job or a relationship that works.

Dreams give us goals, and goals can be broken down into steps which we can measure and which bring our goals – and dreams – closer.

For example, if you long for a happy relationship after several unhappy ones, you might make it your goal to meet new people and take steps towards that, like joining a new club or group. You might also think about your relationship skills, and see a counsellor, or go on a relationship course. Once you achieve your goal and meet new people, you will be so much closer to your dream and you might put in place new goals. When you start dating again, before you know if this is the right person for you or not, you might choose to take things slowly, getting to know them

277

and using your judgement, awareness and self-trust to guide you in the right direction.

I still have big dreams for the Katie Piper Foundation. I want to set up an intensive burns rehabilitation unit like the Centre Ster my doctors referred me to in France. It was a superb centre where I received world-class scar-management therapies. When I see a centre like that open in the UK it will be another big dream ticked off my list.

Keep your dreams alive – and don't tell yourself that they can't come true. Boost your belief in them and your confidence by doing one thing every day to make them happen.

Esteem

You know by now how important self-esteem is to confidence. So keep yours high by being truthful, kind and generous, by listening to others and listening to yourself, too. Give yourself what you need and treat yourself as though you really matter – because you do.

Remember that with high self-esteem you can deal with life's ups and downs so much better. You won't blame yourself when things go wrong and you will like and approve of yourself, no matter what kind of day you have.

Use plenty of positive self-talk, like 'I am a talented, worthwhile person', and don't forget to smile at everyone you meet – smiles melt the hardest hearts.

Remind yourself of all that you have to offer others – at work, at play and in relationships. Value yourself by writing a list of all your qualities and all that you have to offer – make it at least ten points long. When you read it back to yourself you'll find it's hard to feel useless.

No

This little world is your friend and helpmate. If you're anything like me, you're far more familiar with its pal – Yes. But saying yes to everything is exhausting and overwhelming. It makes it impossible to look after yourself properly or give of your best. So start being more selective and saying no more often. You can say it nicely (although be firm, don't dither so that people think you don't really mean it). Phrases like 'I'm afraid I can't' and 'I'm not free that day' or 'can I suggest an alternative?' can be helpful. No comes in many guises, but the other people need to know that you mean it.

If you really find it hard saying no, buy time by saying, 'I'll get back to you when I check my diary'. Then take a deep breath, remember why you're doing it and get back to them with a polite, sorry, no. Far from making you feel bad, once you get the hang of it, no can be the most powerful word in your confidence toolkit.

Contribution

A big part of confidence is feeling that we have something to contribute – to others and to the community or society we live in. When you are making a contribution, you feel worthwhile, and that leads straight to higher confidence levels.

What do I mean by making a contribution? It's being a part of something, having input, giving what you can. When you contribute you help to achieve something. You are part of bringing about a positive outcome, whether that's cakes for the school fair, or the completion of a work project.

To contribute you need to be connected with other people, through a family, a group or a workforce. Making a contribution means playing a worthwhile part in that group of people, being part of something bigger, that you all bring about together. You use your skills and abilities to complement those of other people and your contribution gives your life meaning, depth and purpose.

Energy

Energy is incredibly important – without it we're not good for much, and with it we feel we can achieve anything.

There's a school of thought that says we focus too much on how much time we have, and not enough on how much energy we have. So that when we feel overloaded, rather than simply resigning ourselves to working longer hours, we should re-examine our energy levels and how we are managing them.

I think this is so true. When we have physical, emotional, mental and spiritual energy, it means we are at our best.

For physical energy we need that nurturing self-care, making sure we get enough sleep, healthy food, exercise and rest-breaks. Working flat-out all day isn't always the best use of your energy. A short break in the day, to rest or read, can renew us.

For emotional energy, be creative, spend time with people you love and practise gratitude and appreciation.

For mental energy, use lots of affirmations and positive self-talk and look for opportunities to contribute.

For spiritual energy, find sources of shared values, beliefs and purpose. This may be through a group or community, and through doing work that you feel really matters and makes a difference.

Treat your energy like a valuable resource, because while you can't do much about how many hours there are in the day, you can make a huge difference to the levels of energy that you have during those hours.

The message I want to leave with you is that your confidence is in your own hands. You don't have to look to anyone else for the resources and tools you need to build and maintain genuine confidence. And with high confidence levels, the world is yours. To me, having consistent high-level confidence is as good as winning the lottery or climbing Everest, except the odds of achieving it are a whole lot better.

What I have learned on my journey of recovery, and through all of the amazing people I have met along the way, is that nothing can break the human spirit. We can cope with all kinds of traumas and heartaches, our bodies can be shattered, but there is something within the human spirit that remains strong and helps us to survive, to overcome adversity and to triumph.

And I don't know about you, but that makes me feel confident.

Bibliography

Eating Disorders

There is a great deal of help out there now for people who have eating disorders, and also for their friends and family. Here are some suggestions:

Books
Anorexia Nervosa, Janet Treasure and June Alexander (Routledge, paperback/ebook)

Overcoming Anorexia, Professor J Hubert Lacy (Sheldon, paperback/ebook)

Overcoming Anorexia Nervosa, Christopher Freeman (Robinson, paperback/ebook)

Overcoming Binge Eating (2nd edition), Dr Christopher Fairburn (Guilford Press, hardback/ebook)

Overcoming Bulimia Nervosa and Binge-Eating (New revised edition), Peter Cooper (Robinson, paperback/ebook)

Getting Better Bite by Bite: A Survival Kit for Sufferers of Bulimia Nervosa and Binge Eating Disorders, Ulrike Schmidt, Janet Treasure and June Alexander (Routledge, paperback/ebook)

Other Resources

Beat – the UK's leading charity supporting anyone affected by eating disorders: www.b-eat.co.uk

Fact sheet on eating disorders from the Royal College of Psychiatrists: www.rcpsych.ac.uk/healthadvice/problemsdisorders/eatingdisorderskeyfacts.aspx

Fact sheet on eating disorders by Christine Webber on the Netdoctor website: www.netdoctor.co.uk/conditions/brain-and-nervous-system/a11609/eating-disorders/

Cognitive Behavioural Therapy (CBT)

Books

Cognitive Behavioural Therapy for Dummies, Rhena Branch (For Dummies, paperback/ebook)

Mind Over Mood, Dennis Greenberger and Christine Padesky (Guilford Press, paperback/ebook)

Life Coaching: A Cognitive-Behavioural Approach (2nd edition), Michael Neenan and Windy Dryden (Routledge, paperback/ebook)

Developing Resilience: A Cognitive-Behavioural Approach, Michael Neenan (Routledge, paperback/ebook)

Other Resources

Living Life to the Full – A free-to-use website with helpful courses and strategies designed by a highly experienced CBT psychiatrist: www.llttf.com

An excellent introduction to CBT on the Royal College of Psychiatrists website:

www.rcpsych.ac.uk/mentalhealthinformation/therapies/cogni-tivebehaviou#raltherapy.aspx

NEW FROM KATIE PIPER IN MARCH 2018

Join Katie Piper in this inspiring book
on raising a daughter in the modern world

Whether you're becoming a mum for the first time or you have children who are growing up faster than you could have ever imagined, motherhood can feel like the most joyful and yet the most daunting of times. But you're not alone.

This is my journey in motherhood: my experiences, hopes and fears and a parenting expert's empowering advice to guide you from those first wobbly moments to being a happy, healthy mum, raising feisty, independent children who aren't afraid to be themselves.

Katie Piper

From Mother to Daughter is about motherhood, what you learn as a mother and the things you would tell your daughter. But most of all it's a celebration of the incredible power of mother–daughter relationships.